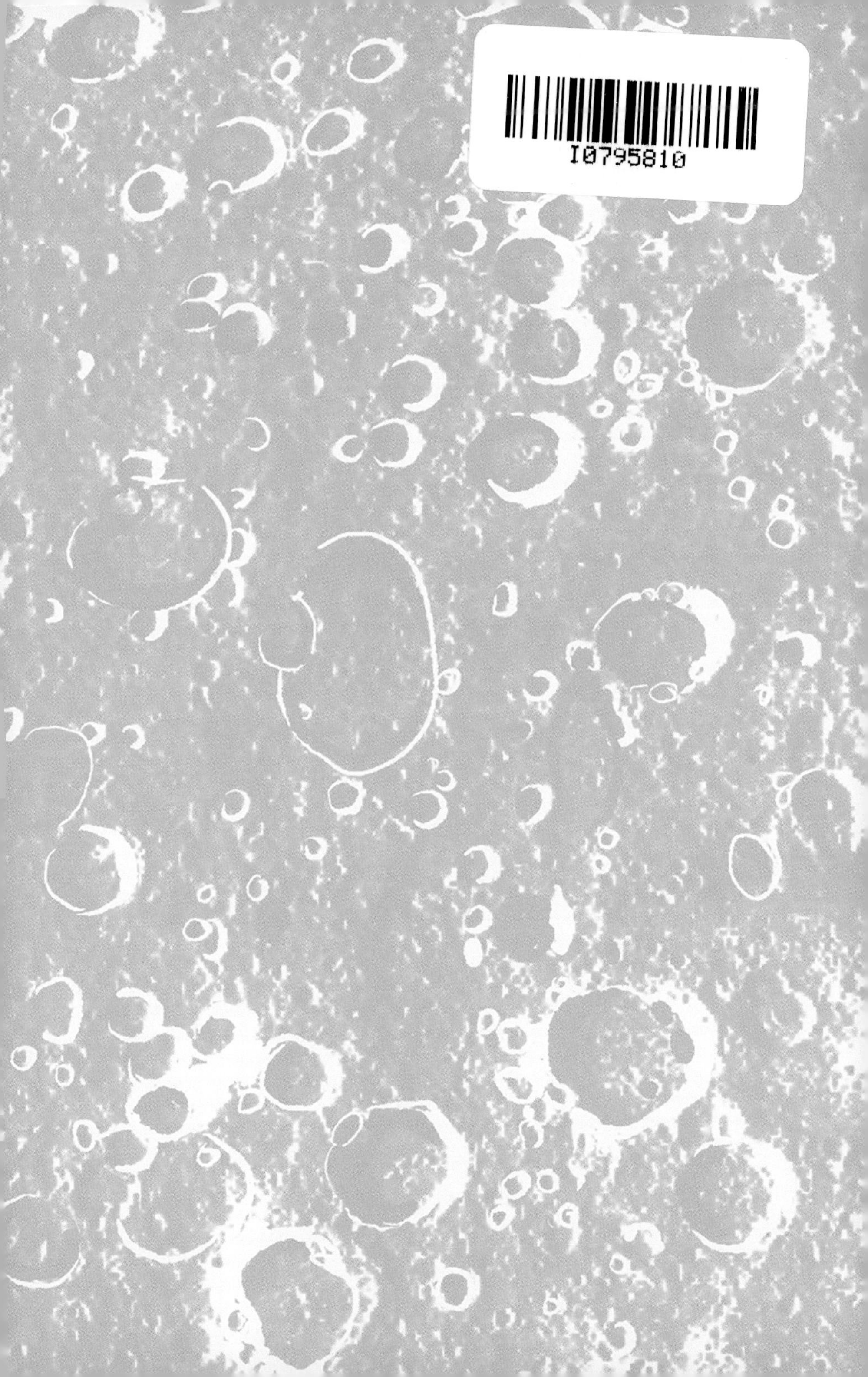

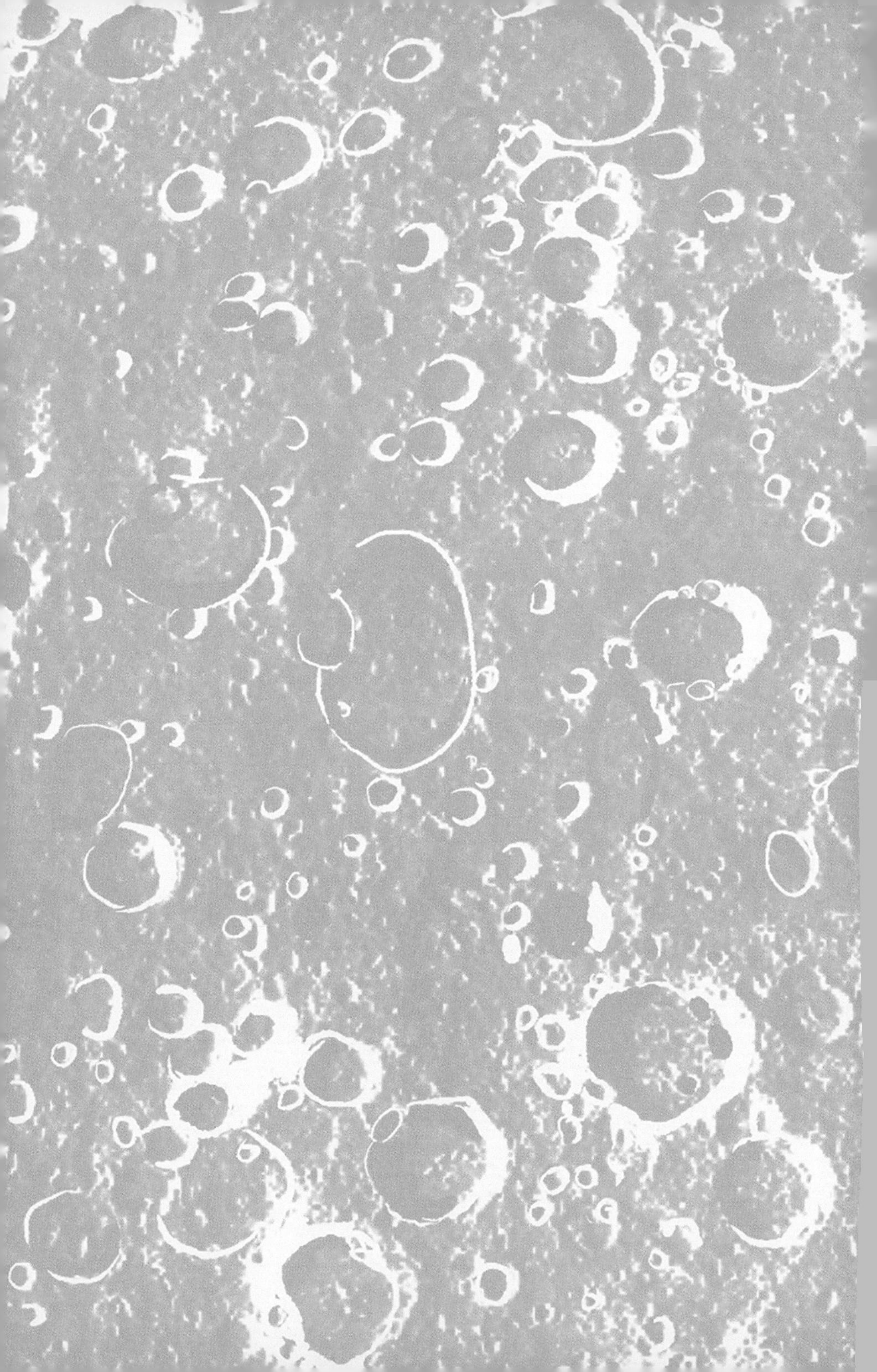

MOON LANDING

Written by Stephen Krensky
Illustrated by Greta Samuel

Author's note

This is a retelling of real-life events surrounding the Apollo 11 mission. It is based particularly on the mission logs and the astronauts' own recollections. While staying true to the facts, some imagination has been used to bring the story to life.

DK would like to thank NASA and US Navy for images that were used as references to create some of the artworks in this book.

First American Edition, 2026
Published in the United States by DK Publishing,
a division of Penguin Random House LLC
1745 Broadway, 20th Floor, New York, NY 10019

26 27 28 29 30 10 9 8 7 6 5 4 3 2
005–352505–Mar/2026

Published in Great Britain by Dorling Kindersley Limited

ISBN: 979-8-2171-3415-1

DK books are available at special discounts when purchased in bulk for sales promotions, premiums, fund-raising, or educational use.
For details, contact: DK Publishing Special Markets,
1745 Broadway, 20th Floor, New York, NY 10019
SpecialSales@dk.com

Printed and bound in China

www.dk.com

FSC www.fsc.org MIX Paper FSC™ C018179

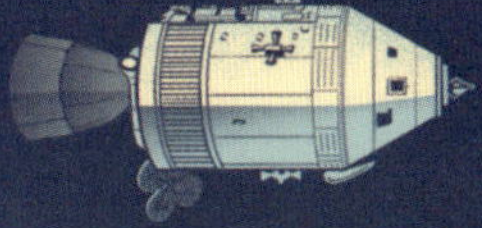

CONTENTS

UNITED STATES

CHAPTER ONE
LIFTOFF!

July 16, 1969, Cape Kennedy, Florida

"T-minus 60 seconds …"

The voice of launch commentator, Jack King, booms out over the loudspeakers. The day is sunny and pleasantly warm. Only a few high scattered clouds overhead interrupt the deep blue sky.

Almost a million spectators are listening to these dramatic words. They have gathered near the Kennedy Space Center in Florida hoping to witness the start of an historic event—the flight of Apollo 11 and its quest to put the first human beings on the Moon.

These people have arrived on foot and bicycles, in sedans and station wagons, RVs and motorcycles. They have filled the tiered seating at the Space Center's viewing areas, and gathered on the beach, the shoulder of US 1, and the shore of the Indian River. They are sitting on car hoods and holding bulky 35mm cameras. Some have camped out overnight to claim a good spot.

Everywhere the mood is friendly and excited. Just a hint of tension simmers below the surface, a hint that reflects the uncertainty of not knowing exactly what will happen next.

All eyes, whether shaded by sunglasses or aided by binoculars and telescopes, are trained on the 363-foot-tall Saturn V rocket, which sits 3 miles away like a lonely skyscraper rising from the flat and scrubby landscape. Why so far? To keep spectators safe from the coming eruption of heat, hot gases, and thunderous noise when the launch begins. And should the worst happen, should there be an explosion—one that would generate the same power as a small nuclear blast—they are at a safe distance to survive that, too.

The rocket is gleaming white with black stripes marking its three stages. It appears rooted to the concrete pad beneath it, anchored by its own enormous weight and held in place by the nine swing arms of the giant metal service tower that stands beside it.

The launchpad is deserted. All the workers have retreated to safety. The deep mechanical hum of the huge pumps feeding super-cooled liquid into the rocket's gigantic hydrogen and oxygen tanks is now silent, the tanks full. The only living creatures nearby are a few indifferent seagulls, wheeling around the top of the rocket.

PERCHED ON THE VERY TOP OF THE ROCKET, LIKE A TINY BEAK ON THE HEAD OF A GIGANTIC BIRD, IS THE APOLLO 11 CAPSULE

The Saturn V is the biggest rocket ever built. It is four times taller and a hundred times more powerful than the Mercury booster that launched Alan Shepard, the first American astronaut, into space just eight years earlier. Fully fueled, it holds almost 1 million gallons of kerosene, liquid oxygen, and liquid hydrogen, which will generate the huge amount of thrust needed to break free of Earth's gravity and carry the rocket's precious payload beyond Earth's orbit.

The rocket is made up of three parts, called stages, each with its own fuel tanks and engines. These stages must fire up in turn. When the fuel in one stage is used up, the empty tank and its engines will separate and fall away, and the engines on the next stage will fire up. In this way the rocket will reduce its weight and increase its speed as it climbs higher and higher, and set the spacecraft on its course to the Moon.

Perched on the very top of the rocket, like a tiny beak on the head of a gigantic bird, is the Apollo 11 Command Module capsule. It is just 9 feet tall and 13 feet wide, about the same size as a large car. Inside are the astronauts chosen for this crew—Mission Commander Neil Armstrong, Lunar Module Pilot Buzz Aldrin, and Command Module Pilot Michael Collins.

Neil Armstrong has always had flying in his blood. He took his first airplane flight as a six-year-old. Ten years later he earned a pilot's license—before he even learned to drive a car. Neil has flown over 200 kinds of planes during his career. A test pilot in the 1950s, he became an astronaut in 1962. Known for his cool reserve, he cheated death the year before by ejecting out of a faulty aircraft only moments before it crashed—and then calmly returned to the office to fill out the necessary paperwork.

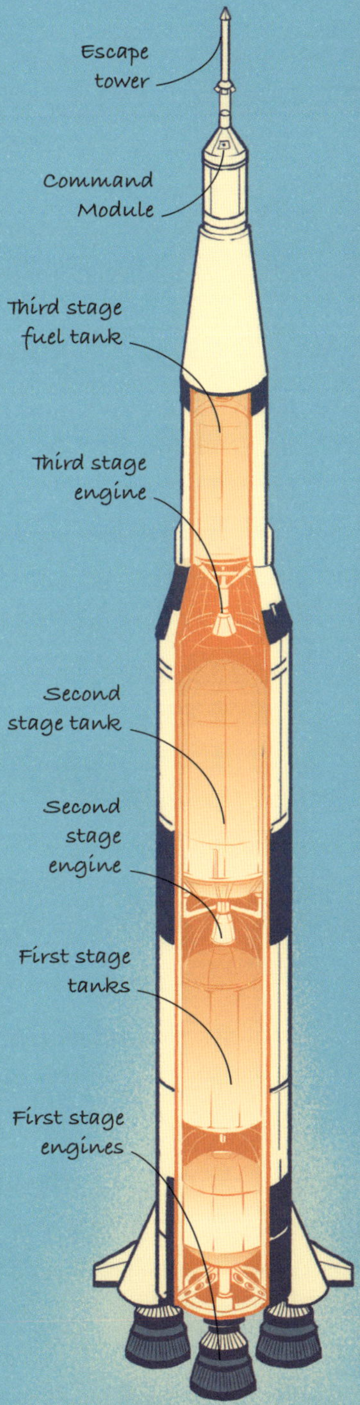

Edwin Aldrin is that rare combination of scholar and pilot. Everyone calls him Buzz—it's a childhood nickname that stuck. A graduate of the United States Military Academy, he later earned a doctorate in astronautics. Buzz overcame early cases of motion sickness to earn his rock-steady reputation as a combat pilot in the Korean War. He joined the astronaut corps in 1963 and flew into space on the final Gemini mission, Gemini 12.

Mike Collins is an army brat, the son of a two-star general, who grew up in six different military posts from Italy to Oklahoma. After graduating from the US Military Academy, he joined the air force and became a test pilot. As a former Gemini astronaut, Mike has spacewalked several times. He knows what it means to be truly alone in space.

All three men are well aware that nothing about their flight is a given. Only eight years have passed since President John F. Kennedy proclaimed the dramatic goal of landing a man on the Moon and

then returning him safely to Earth before the end of the decade. "We choose to go to the Moon," he famously said, "not because it is easy but because it is hard." And "hard," as everyone understands without anybody saying it alone, also means "dangerous."

"WE CHOOSE TO GO TO THE MOON NOT BECAUSE IT IS EASY BUT BECAUSE IT IS HARD"

Kennedy's inspiring speech is a brave call for the United States. After all, the US is not the only nation exploring the stars. Another country, the Soviet Union, has also been grabbing the headlines. Both of them are locked in a deadly serious cold war for world leadership. Exploring outer space is part of this battleground, and the Soviet Union has already won two early victories. It was the first to send a satellite into space and then later a man into orbit. Since then, though, the momentum has shifted. The United States now leads in the space race, but there is no room to take that lead for granted.

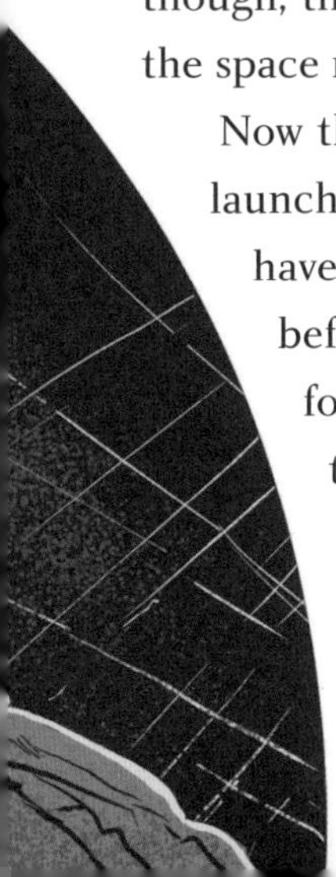

Now the days, hours, minutes, and even the seconds before the launch of Apollo 11 have almost all fallen away. Years of planning have led to this morning, not just from the Apollo missions before this one, but the 12 two-man Gemini missions they followed, and the seven solo Mercury ones that came before that. Each voyage contributed vital steps toward the dream of finally setting foot on the Moon.

"40 seconds away from the Apollo 11 liftoff ..."

On board the capsule, it's a tight fit for everyone. Cocooned in their thick spacesuits, the three astronauts are strapped tightly into their seats. There is no room to spare. Their elbows are touching. If anyone gets an itch, scratching it is going to be a problem.

However nervous the astronauts may be, they aren't showing it. In front of them are panels full of different controls, including hundreds of switches, banks of circuit breakers, a cluster of warning lights, and two keyboards directing the computer.

ONE QUICK TWIST OF THE ABORT HANDLE WILL SHOOT THE CAPSULE AWAY FROM THE ROCKET BENEATH THEM

To Neil's left is perhaps the most important device—the abort handle. If he feels their lives are in jeopardy during liftoff, one quick twist will ignite a set of thrusters on the spacecraft, shooting the capsule away from the rocket beneath them. That decision is his as mission commander. The Mercury and Gemini missions used ejection seats to shoot astronauts out of harm's way, but the Saturn V's engines are so big that ejection seats would not carry the astronauts far enough to be safe.

In theory, propelling the whole capsule to a great distance will protect the astronauts inside. But is that true? No one knows for sure because, unlike ejection seats, the abort procedure is considered too dangerous to test. Of course, it will only be used in the worst of emergencies. But on a countdown like this, the worst of emergencies is only a heartbeat away.

"We'll do what we need to do," thinks Neil. But he certainly hopes it's a call he never has to make.

"30 seconds and counting ..."

This isn't Mike's first time sitting on top of a giant rocket about to blast off into space, but still, he is tense. Thousands of people—hundreds of thousands—have spent the last few years working on the Apollo program. Time and again they were told it couldn't be done. The technology had not yet been invented. The needed science was woefully incomplete.

And yet these scientists and mathematicians, administrators and construction workers refused to give up. Their determination sparked their ingenuity, which in turn has brought them to this day.

Mike wants to make these people proud.

About 400 of them are sitting in the nearby Launch Control Center. They are monitoring the rocket, the life-support systems, equipment readiness, and even the weather. The building's reinforced concrete walls and thick glass windows will keep them safe, but it isn't their own safety they are thinking about. Neil, Buzz, and Mike are the ones on everyone's mind. Will this day, July 16, 1969, begin a truly historic mission? Or will there be a mistake? A tragedy? A setback so disastrous that the American space program will never recover?

"20 seconds and counting ..."

Buzz is thinking back in time. The first powered airplane took to the skies in 1903, when the Wright Brothers' flyer first rose above the sandy dunes near Kitty Hawk, North Carolina. Now, only 66 years later here he is embarking on a much longer and more daring voyage through the sky.

As Buzz looks to the south, where some of the former launches took place, his eyes rest on Launchpad 34, now considered hallowed ground. It's been less than three years since his fellow astronauts Gus Grissom, Roger Chaffee, and Ed White were caught in a tragic fire there during a pre-launch training test for Apollo 1. All three died.

There have been other deaths, too, of American test pilots and Russian cosmonauts. But those are in the past. Neil, Buzz, and Mike hope for a happier ending to their flight.

"12, 11, 10, 9—ignition sequence starts …"

Now the Saturn V rocket bursts into life. Steam vents from the powerful engines. Flame and smoke shoot outward from the rocket's base. In the blink of an eye, 23 tons of fuel burn up before the rocket ever leaves the ground.

Sheets of ice, which had gathered on the rocket's outer skin overnight, freezing because of the supercooled liquid oxygen

"THREE, TWO, ONE, ZERO, ALL ENGINES RUNNING. LIFTOFF! LIFTOFF ON APOLLO 11!"

beneath, shatter from the powerful vibrations. The broken shards fall glitteringly to the ground.

Inside, the astronauts exchange nervous grins. Years of training have prepared them for this moment. They've spent thousands of hours practicing every kind of scenario. But this is the real thing. They cannot see what is happening outside their craft, but their bodies shake as the enormous rocket suddenly awakens, like a sleeping giant come to life. The vibration pierces their suits, their skin, and passes right through their bones.

"Three, two, one, zero, all engines running. Liftoff!" says King. "We have a liftoff at 32 minutes past the hour. Liftoff on Apollo 11!"

So much rumbling. So much roaring thunder. It is hard to sense the exact moment of leaving the ground.

"Shake, rattle, and roll!" thinks Mike.

CHAPTER TWO
GOODBYE TO EARTH

Neil, Buzz, and Mike are on the rollercoaster ride of their lives. All five F-1 engines on the Saturn V first stage are firing. The three astronauts are thrown to the left and right and back again.

Outside the spacecraft, the arms of the metal service structure pull back dramatically and the giant clamps at the rocket's base are released.

The rocket is free!

For the first 10 seconds, the Saturn V rises up, seemingly in slow motion, on a growing tail of fire. One foot up, and then another, and then a third. The engines seem to sway—each engine can swivel in order to make tiny course corrections that keep the rocket moving upright. It is critical that they do. If the rocket shifts enough to bump the launch tower, the mission will end abruptly in a ball of fire.

There are no certainties to lean on with a machine that contains 3 million parts. At some point all anyone can do is hope for the best. But that isn't the most comforting thought when your insides and outside feel like the main ingredients being whipped around in a Mixmaster.

The rocket holds its course. It is still moving slowly upward, as if arguing with the forces of gravity to let it go.

"Tower cleared!" says King, his voice both excited and relieved at the same time.

FOR THE FIRST TEN SECONDS, SATURN V RISES UP ON A GROWING TAIL OF FIRE

Inside the capsule, the deafening roar of the launch obliterates all else. Besides the noise coming directly from the 7.5 million pounds of thrust, the echo of that noise is also reflecting off the ground. In these crucial moments, none of the astronauts can hear anything over the radio or from one another. They are very alone. If Flight Command sees a problem, if a sudden emergency appears, the astronauts will never know about it. Until it's too late.

Neil's blood pressure is rising. His heart is pounding. If anything goes wrong—if the speed slows or their direction veers off course—Neil is in charge. He must be prepared to make decisions on the fly.

At 13.2 seconds into the flight, the rocket rolls into its flight trajectory, tilting from the upright 90 degrees of launch to a slanted 72 degrees, the angle needed to put them on the curved path of Earth orbit.

After 30 seconds or so, the noise lessens, and communications are restored.

Now, a new voice speaks into the astronauts' headsets. It is the Capsule Communicator (CAPCOM), one of several designated for this flight. CAPCOM is based at Mission Control in Houston. It is the CAPCOM's job to be the primary voice between the people on the ground—the many flight controllers, scientists, and project engineers—and the three astronauts. They are trained to be clear, concise, and above all calm no matter what is taking place.

This first CAPCOM is Bruce McCandless, a fellow astronaut who is scheduled to fly on later flights in the space program. He announces that Mission Control in Houston is taking over control from the firing command in Florida.

"Apollo 11, this is Houston," says Bruce. "You are go for staging."

Just under three minutes into the flight, 40 miles above Earth's surface, the five F-1 engines on the first stage shut down, their job done. As the rocket suddenly stops accelerating, the three astronauts are thrown forward hard. The first stage of the rocket, engines and

USA

all, separates from the rest of the spacecraft. Its fuel gone, it falls away, soon to splash down harmlessly into the Atlantic Ocean.

A few seconds later Neil reports that they have achieved skirt separation. The skirt is the structure that connects the first and second stages of the rocket. After the first stage is jettisoned, the interstage skirt is also released. Once it is gone, the second stage engine can ignite.

THE FIRST STAGE OF THE ROCKET, ENGINES AND ALL, SEPARATES FROM THE REST OF THE SPACECRAFT

"And ignition," says Neil.

"Thrust is go, all engines," says Bruce. "You're looking good."

The five J-2 engines on the second stage spring to life. They may not roar as loudly as the F-1s before them, but they are powerful nonetheless. Apollo 11 is now traveling at 6,500 miles per hour. The air, the clouds, the blue sky, are officially behind them. At 45 miles up, the spacecraft is now seven times higher than most commercial jets will ever fly.

The escape rocket that Neil was controlling with his abort handle is now released, that danger having passed. The escape tower takes with it the protective shield covering the front of the capsule.

"They finally gave me a window to look out!" says Mike.

Not that there is much to see, since the window is pointing up into the inky blackness of space. Now 60 miles up, and the last vestiges of the atmosphere, the thin blanket of gases that protect the Earth from cosmic rays and other harmful radiation, have faded away. This is the point at which space truly begins.

For the next nine minutes, the second stage engines burn bright. Faster and faster, the capsule hurls onward. The G-forces that measure acceleration are building fast. These forces create an intense pressure that pushes down against the astronauts. It feels as though an elephant is sitting on their chests.

Then the engines shut down. Their flames are extinguished. The blackness pulls in close again, enveloping the ship. The astronauts feel the abrupt deceleration as their seat restraints again take the strain. Then the entire second stage is released to fall back to Earth.

Now more than 100 miles above Earth, the third stage engine ignites for the first time. Flames cut through the darkness, a tiny point of light brightening the surrounding area.

Unlike its bigger brothers, this engine is designed to work more than once. As it burns this first time, the ride in the capsule becomes a little rougher. This last stage of the rocket must give one final kick to accelerate Apollo 11 to 17,500 miles per hour.

When the engine shuts down almost three minutes later, Apollo 11 is in a stable orbit 115 miles above Earth's surface. The planet's gravity still tugs on the spacecraft, but it is now traveling fast enough that it can stop accelerating. Instead of being pulled down, the craft and its crew will keep flying in a curved path around Earth. Being above the atmosphere there is no air to slow them down, so they maintain their speed even though no engine is firing.

With the launch safely past, Neil, Buzz, and Mike exchange smiles, but there are no high fives in space. Their journey is just beginning.

CHAPTER THREE
HAVING A BLAST

The Earth looms large below Apollo 11 as it continues on its silent path around the planet. In the next three hours, the crew will travel one and a half orbits around Earth. They need this time to make sure all systems are functioning properly. There is little margin for error. After that, they will fire up the third stage engine for the second time—to send them on their way to the Moon.

Whatever they need to accomplish now, they will be doing it while experiencing weightlessness. When they unclip their restraints, the astronauts float out of their seats. Now that they are no longer accelerating but traveling at a constant speed, the G-forces they were feeling have gone. Earth's gravity is still there pulling on them, but in orbit they don't feel its effects.

Even after countless hours of practice, training underwater in pressure suits, nothing can really prepare them for the sensation of being weightless. It's disconcerting. Not only does the body float, but fluids inside the body act differently, obeying different rhythms. It's common to feel dizzy or lightheaded. Sudden fatigue is also a risk. So, the astronauts must move slowly and not wiggle their heads too much.

Neil, Buzz, and Mike are prepared. They are trained to deal with these challenges. However, that doesn't mean they are immune to the uncomfortable feelings that crop up. It just means being uncomfortable sometimes is the way things are.

And the potential problems are not just internal ones. Tools that might be left out for a moment may start drifting away. Anything that

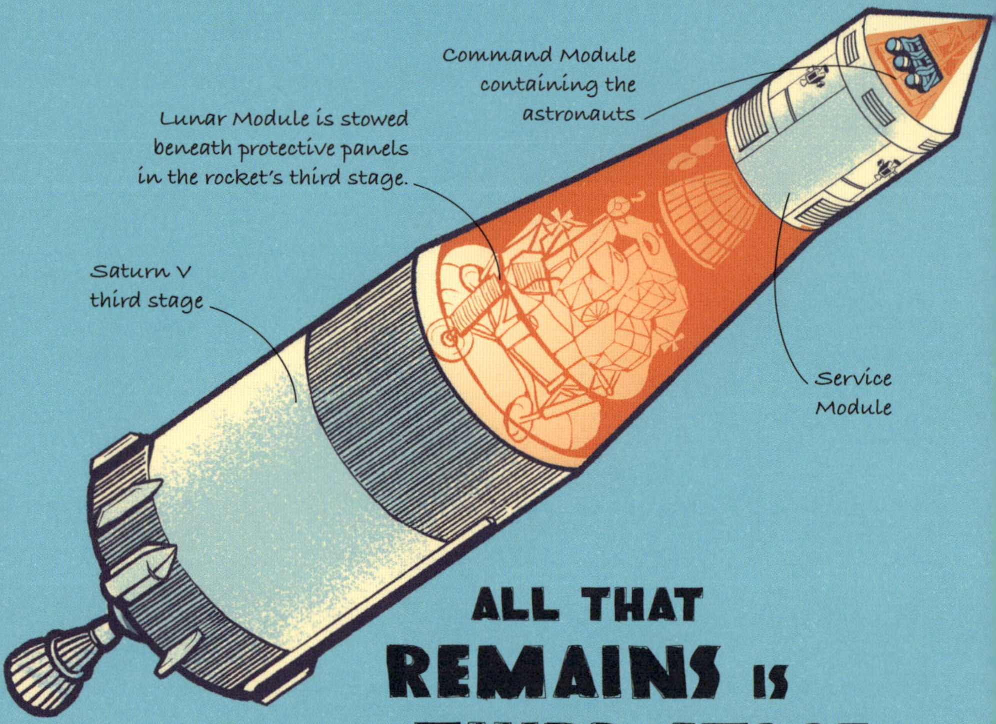

ALL THAT REMAINS IS THE THIRD STAGE

needs to stay put will have to be held down. Buzz watches a pencil float by as he gets down to work.

Below them, Earth is a bluish marble set against the inky blackness of space. But while space remains as big as ever, the spacecraft itself has become smaller. All that remains of the Saturn V is the third stage and its precious spacecraft payload. Without its first and second stages, it looks like the top of a shiny pencil. The cone-shaped Command Module is the tip, containing the cramped crew compartment. Underneath it is the cylindrical Service Module, which holds fuel cells, power systems, oxygen and hydrogen storage tanks, and other supplies. The Lunar Module—the craft that will actually take Neil and Buzz to the Moon's surface—is safely stored away inside the top of the rocket's third stage.

The three astronauts begin moving about in the Command Module. Like sardines in a can, they are packed in pretty tightly. Still, they do their best to avoid bumping into one another.

"After you," says Neil, beckoning Buzz ahead.

"No, no," says Buzz. 'You go first, commander. I insist."

Mike floats down to the equipment bay to look at the navigation system tucked beneath the crew couches. As Command Module Pilot, he needs to be absolutely sure they are where they are supposed to be at the exact time they are supposed to be there. Some of the navigational information is collected from instruments on board. Other bits and pieces are added from tracking stations on Earth, stations that are teaming up to continuously follow Apollo 11's location.

Although he trusts the computers to keep track of things, Mike still relies on a sextant to confirm their location. Sailors on the high seas have used sextants since the 1700s to determine their position out of sight of land, by using the stars to navigate.

A traditional sextant is a small tool with an eyepiece, internal mirrors, and adjustable metal arms, which measures the angle between the horizon and a star. Mike's is a little more complicated than the traditional ones, but the principles are the same. It is mounted into the side of the craft, and Mike looks through an eyepiece to measure the positions of distant stars. He checks his reading against where the computer says the star should be. In this way he knows whether or not they are on track.

"Are we lost?" asks Buzz. "I'm sure there's somewhere nearby we can ask for directions."

"I'll keep that in mind," says Mike. "But we're fine for now."

Once Mike has reassured himself about their position, he can take a moment to look at the view. The planet below is cloaked in darkness but he senses the dawn approaching. "Stand by for sunrise!" he says.

A BLAZE OF LIGHT PIERCES THE BLACKNESS AS THE SUN BURSTS OVER THE HORIZON

Outside the window a gray glimmer is shimmering around the edge of the globe. In the next moment, a jagged blaze of light pierces the blackness as the Sun bursts over the horizon. It's an awe-inspiring sight. The terminator—the line that marks the boundary between day and night, one side in darkness the other in the light—sweeps swiftly across the globe as the star rises above the horizon, bathing more and more of the planet in light.

"Isn't that something?" says Neil. "Get a picture!"

Unfortunately, their state-of-the-art camera, a Hasselblad, is nowhere to be found.

"Has anybody seen a Hasselblad floating by?" asks Mike. "It couldn't have gone very far, big son of a gun like that … Everybody look for a floating Hasselblad. I see a pen floating loose down here, too. Is anybody missing a ballpoint pen?"

"Got mine," says Buzz.

"I've looked everywhere over here for that Hasselblad," says Mike,

Hasselblad camera

"and I just don't see it … Ah! Here it is … It was floating in the aft bulkhead."

With that mystery solved, the astronauts get back to their checklists. Everything must be shipshape before the next phase of the mission starts. Hardware and software are checked and rechecked. And then checked again. Flight controllers in Houston must be absolutely sure that the Command Module and the Lunar Module can perform properly. The Command Module has over 2 million parts. All of them were inspected many times before the launch, but that was then. This is now. Has the liftoff affected the equipment? Is anything damaged or broken?

Eventually, everyone is satisfied. They are ready for the next milestone in their journey. Houston shares this conclusion. "Apollo 11, you are go for TLI."

TLI stands for trans-lunar injection and it is a critical moment in the flight. This is the point when they will change their trajectory from a stable orbit around Earth to a path toward the Moon.

It is not enough to just point the spacecraft toward the Moon, fire up the engine, and hope for the best. Nothing in space stays in one place. Where the Moon is now is not where it will be when Apollo 11 gets to it in a few days. The Moon is always on the move, orbiting around Earth. So, everything has to be reckoned with a precise timetable for the engine burn. If all goes to plan, their path will take them to a lunar orbit, where the Moon's gravity will capture the spacecraft. Even a little bit off course and they will miss the Moon entirely and continue on into outer space with no way to get home.

"Ignition!" says Neil.

The engine comes alive again with a burst of bright flame. Outside the spacecraft, the hydrogen fuel is burning brightly, leaving a trail of pink and purple fire behind it.

"Trajectory and guidance look good," says Houston.

"Roger," says Neil. His voice is calm, and his jaw unclenches a little. As far as he can tell, nothing is wrong. But it doesn't hurt to have the experts at home confirm these impressions, even if they are more than 100 very long miles away.

A few seconds later, Flight Control is back. "Apollo 11, this is Houston … You're still looking good. Your predicted cutoff is right on the nominal."

"Nominal" is a fancy engineering way to say normal.

When the burn ends, Apollo 11 is powering toward the Moon.

"Hey, Houston," says Neil, "that Saturn gave us a magnificent ride."

As it leaves Earth behind, the Apollo 11 spacecraft is more alone than ever, the tiniest grain of sand in the beach that is the Solar System. It is now moving at 24,500 miles per hour—more than 10 times faster than a speeding bullet.

But even at that speed, they're just getting started.

CHAPTER FOUR
DANCING IN SPACE

For the three Apollo 11 astronauts, time is relative. They have already accomplished a lot and dodged a number of possible calamities. It is almost hard to believe that only a little over three hours have passed since they blasted off.

The next box to be checked off on their schedule is a big one. So far, the Lunar Module has been a hitchhiker on the flight, tucked up inside the rocket's third stage. Taking the Lunar Module out of storage and docking it with the Command and Service Module (CSM) is tricky. It's not like a giant hand can just open the top and pull the Lunar Module out. Mike will need all his expertise to move

the CSM away from the third stage, turn it around, then dock with the Lunar Module so the two craft are joined together. This tricky piece of flying is called the Transposition and Docking Maneuver.

"Apollo 11, you're go for separation."

"Okay, Houston," says Neil, "we're about to sep."

Mike flicks a switch, blowing the explosive bolts that connect the CSM to the third stage.

Neil and Buzz feel the bolts firing and hear the metal clanging outside the ship. The sound is a bit unsettling. It's a noise that suggests something is broken or damaged even though it's what they expect to hear. The protective panels housing the Lunar Module have been released and drift off into space. With that, Mike makes his move.

As the CSM and the third stage drift apart, Mike briefly turns on the thrusters. The extra boost sends the CSM about 100 feet ahead of the third stage. That's the distance Mike needs. Now he slowly rotates the CSM a full 180 degrees. Once this U-turn is complete, Mike looks back at the Lunar Module sitting inside the third stage.

Nose to nose.

All of this takes place against the spectacular backdrop of the distant Pacific Ocean, but Mike is concentrating hard. He has no time to enjoy the view.

Mike has practiced this maneuver hundreds of times in the simulator. He knows how to make the approach, how to gradually bring the two vehicles together. The maneuver will end, he hopes, with a gentle nudge, a little push, and a final click into place. Mike's goal here is not to show off or do some fancy flying. He just wants things to go as smoothly as possible. But that's easier said than done—especially when everyone and everything is traveling at more than 20,000 miles per hour.

SLOWLY, CAREFULLY, MIKE NUDGES HIS SHIP CLOSER AND CLOSER

Slowly, carefully, Mike nudges his ship closer and closer.

"Don't be shy," he says softly.

He is aiming for the docking port at the top of the Lunar Module. The challenge is to slide the probe on top of the CSM into the port with just enough force. Too gentle and he will miss his mark. Too much force and something may break. The goal is to be like two partners dancing in space. They must work together to find the right rhythm. And when they're done, they'll be locked in step.

Mike is looking through the side window, eyeing the Lunar Module. The window has markings, like the crosshairs on a gunsight. Mike must maneuver his spacecraft until the Lunar Module, still sheltering inside the remains of the Saturn V, is in the crosshairs.

"The LM looks like a mechanical tarantula crouched in its hole," he thinks. "Its one black eye is peering at me."

Luckily, Mike is not afraid of spiders.

"Gently, gently," the other two astronauts are thinking. The Lunar Module is delicate. If Mike comes in at slightly the wrong angle or a little too fast, he could break it. Even a simple dent could cause big problems later on.

After all, there are no repair shops in space.

Mike applies more thrust, a few feet at a time.

"Beautiful!" says Neil.

Buzz agrees. "It really looks nice, doesn't it?"

CLANK!

The CSM and the Lunar Module have met. But it's not exactly the gentle sound Mike was hoping for.

Both ships rock from the impact and then are still. Mike knows he must wait patiently for a while. There is no way the ships can meet together in a perfect line. They need to settle into place. And once they do, Mike is ready. He activates the docking latches.

They snap closed, gripping the two craft in a tight hug.

"We are docked," Neil tells Houston.

"LM looks to be in pretty fine shape," Buzz laughs. The LM is hardly an imposing vehicle. "It looks," he thinks, "like an upside-down cement mixer covered in gold foil."

Buzz is right that there is nothing sleek or futuristic about the Lunar Module's design. The outside is mostly made of an aluminum alloy covered with a thermal blanket and a micrometeoroid shield. Its spindly legs stick out in an almost rickety fashion. The spidery-looking craft is designed to be as light as possible to lessen its need for power and fuel. For this reason, it is neither bulky nor thick, though it still weighs over 33,000 pounds. Only 23 feet high and 31 feet wide, it has a pressurized cabin of 235 cubic feet, about the same as four refrigerators put together.

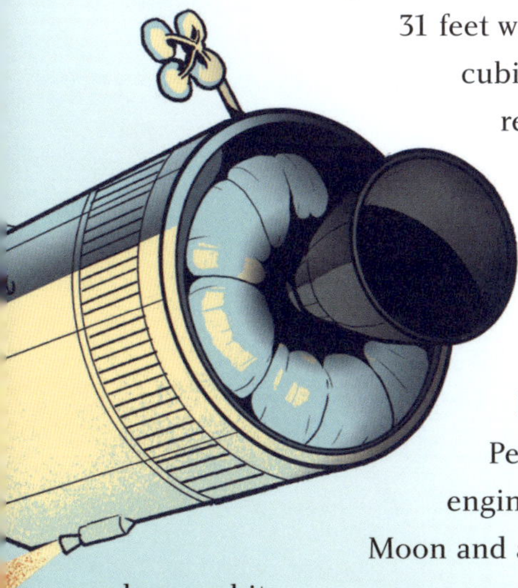

Besides its two passengers, the Lunar Module has room to store life-support backpacks, some equipment to use on the Moon's surface, various tools, and storage batteries that provide electricity. Perhaps most importantly, it has two engines, a larger one for landing on the Moon and a smaller one to power the return to a lunar orbit.

Mike doesn't care what anything looks like. He only wants to make sure nothing has gone wrong. He can't help shaking his head. "Not the smoothest docking I've ever done."

"Well, it feels good from here," says Neil.

It's not just a question of pride for Mike. Even though the docking was successful, he worries that the maneuver has used too much fuel. They can't afford to do that, at least not very often, if they hope to get back home safely. After all, there are no gas stations in space, either.

Still, everything is going according to plan. The CSM is now flying backward, towing the Lunar Module like a car pulling a trailer. And it will keep doing that all the way to the Moon.

With the two modules connected, the third stage of the rocket has now served its last purpose. It plows onward, out of harm's way on a long trip around the Sun.

For the first time during the flight, Neil allows himself to relax enough to take in the view.

"Houston," he says, taking in the view from his small window, "I can observe the entire continent of North America … down to the Yucatán

THEY ARE NOW FLYING BACKWARD, TOWING THE LUNAR MODULE LIKE A CAR PULLING A TRAILER

Peninsula, Cuba, the northern part of South America before I run out of window."

If Mission Control is impressed, they manage to hide it well.

"Roger, we copy."

Neil laughs. He knows the team on the ground has better things to do than listen to him play tour guide. But it's hard not to share some of the excitement he's feeling.

Mike has one more important adjustment to make. They have been flying straight for some time, meaning that one side of the spacecraft has been constantly facing the Sun while the other side has stayed in darkness. The issue isn't between light and dark, though. It's between heat and cold. In space, the Sun will actually broil one side of the ship—and everything in it—if it is exposed to the Sun that way for too long.

Meanwhile, the other side will get unbearably cold.

How to avoid these two extremes? Well, if the ship had the room, it could use bulky heating and cooling equipment to keep everything at a comfortable temperature. Unfortunately, the CSM doesn't have that luxury.

So, the designers came up with a different solution. The engineers call it the Passive Thermal Control (PTC). The astronauts have another name for it—barbecue mode. That's because the PTC causes the ship to slowly rotate, like the rotisserie on a barbecue. As long as the ship maintains a slow but steady spin, the Sun's heat will distribute evenly on all sides.

Once Mike establishes the gentle roll, all three astronauts are happy to shed their protective suits for much more comfortable lighter flight suits.

"Time for dinner," says Neil.

"I hope they haven't lost our reservation," adds Buzz.

There's no need to worry about that in the most exclusive restaurant in the Solar System. The astronauts can now enjoy a peaceful, if not entirely tasty, meal. Their food is pre-measured and pre-packaged—freeze-dried and vacuum-packed in plastic bags—and they have to mix it with water before eating it. But there are main courses like beef with vegetables and chicken and rice. And for dessert? Sugar cookie cubes and fruitcake.

FOR DESSERT? SUGAR COOKIE CUBES AND FRUITCAKE

Eating in space requires a fair amount of attention. If anyone neglects his food for a moment, it may just rise up and wander off. So, it's good to keep an eye on things. The crew can eat solid food straight out of the packet, but anything liquid that requires a spoon can float around in globs if it's left on its own. As for crumbs, they flutter through the air like tiny snowflakes until they are pulled in.

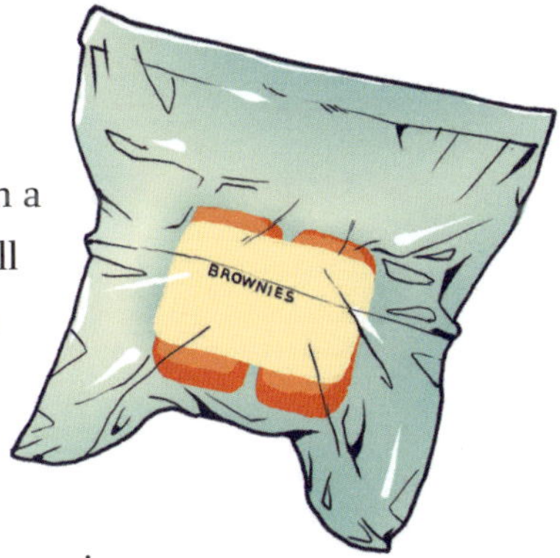

This first meal may not rival fine dining in a fancy restaurant, but no one complains. All the food is a big improvement on the Gemini missions, when eating often meant squeezing nutritious goo out of something that resembled a tube of toothpaste.

Small comforts matter because the voyage is really just starting, and the hours can pass slowly. Listening to music is perhaps the best way to relax considering the close quarters for everyone involved. Neil, Buzz, and Mike each have audio cassettes with their own favorite songs included.

As they listen, the Moon seems to grow larger in front of them. The vastness of space, though, does not seem to change at all.

15,000 miles down. Just 239,000 miles to go.

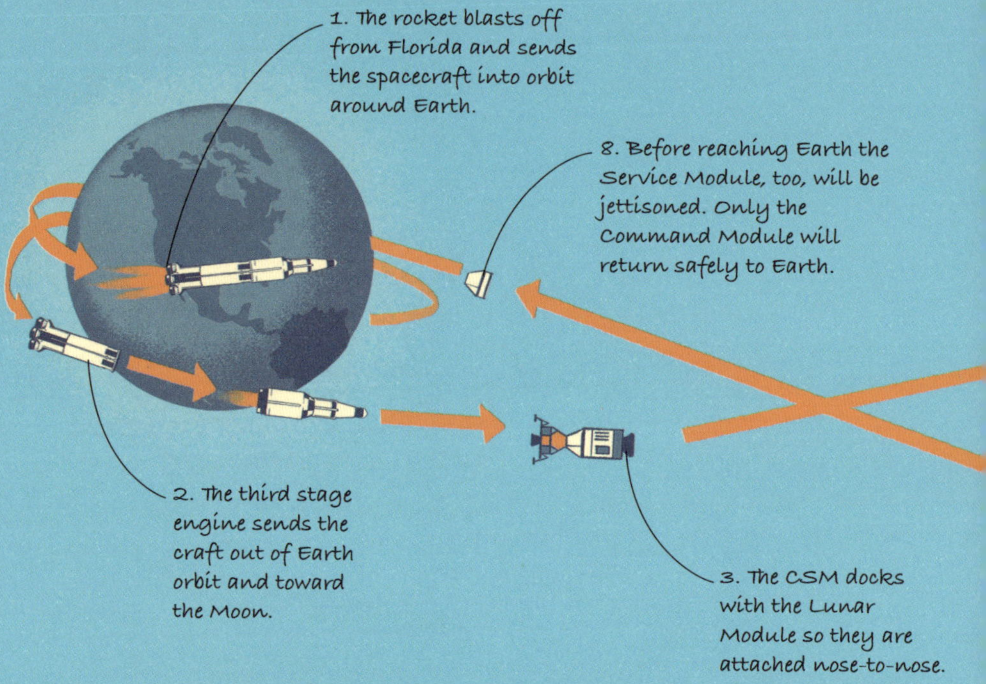

JOURNEY TO THE MOON

Apollo 11's flight plan is a giant figure-eight. After the crew fires the engine to set them on their path toward the Moon they will travel without using any fuel until the Moon's gravity begins to pull them in. Then they will fire the engine again to go into orbit around the Moon. If they for any reason they can't get into orbit around the Moon, their path will send them back toward Earth without having to use any fuel. This plan is called a "free return trajectory."

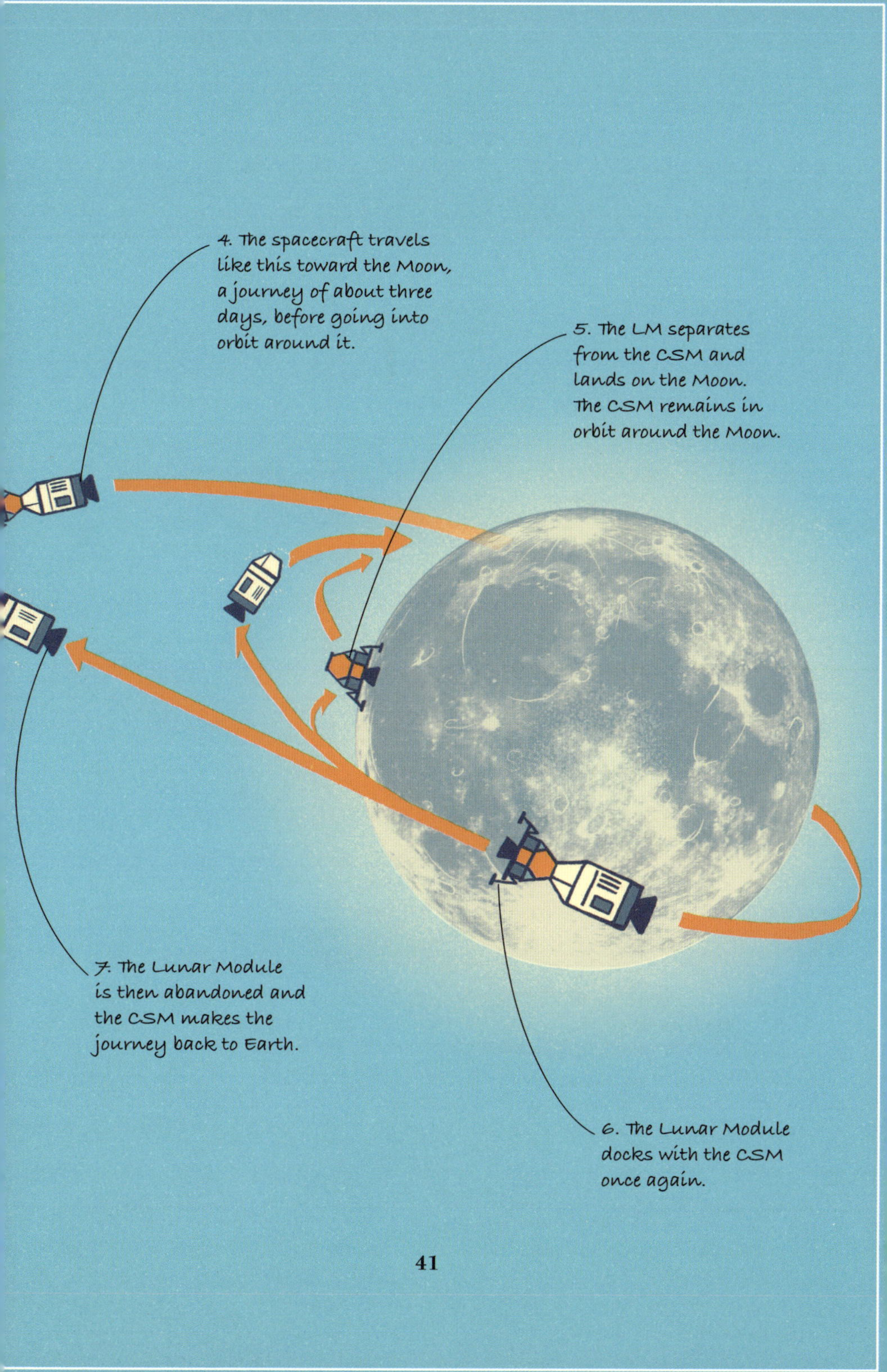
4. The spacecraft travels like this toward the Moon, a journey of about three days, before going into orbit around it.
5. The LM separates from the CSM and lands on the Moon. The CSM remains in orbit around the Moon.
7. The Lunar Module is then abandoned and the CSM makes the journey back to Earth.
6. The Lunar Module docks with the CSM once again.

CHAPTER FIVE
EARTHSHINE

It is quiet on board Apollo 11.

Very quiet.

After an exhausting 11 hours, all three astronauts are fast asleep. They are zipped into their sleep restraints to keep them from floating above their couches. Mission Control is monitoring their life signs, but there isn't anything new to report.

Thump-thump. Thump-thump.

Biometric sensors show slowed heartbeats and regular pulses. Their capsule continues on its way.

When the astronauts awake, about 10 hours later, they are feeling refreshed, and find themselves more than 90,000 miles from home.

"Good morning, Houston. Apollo 11," says Buzz.

"Roger, Apollo 11," says Bruce. "Good morning."

Some housekeeping chores follow—charging batteries, calibrating optics, and dumping some wastewater. With those duties accounted

for, Mike sits again in the pilot's seat, ready to make a midcourse correction burn. This means firing up the CSM's engine to create the right amount of thrust for exactly the right amount of time. The burn takes less than three seconds, but it is crucial. Those few seconds change the capsule's course so they will arrive at a lunar orbit a neighborly 69 miles above the Moon's surface, rather than the distant 201 miles they are currently headed for.

"Houston, burn completed," says Neil.

"That's affirmative," says Bruce from the ground.

With everything running smoothly, Neil takes a moment to look back at Earth. The farther away they are, the more he appreciates what he sees.

They are now so distant, he can take in the whole globe in one glance. The pale blue-and-white sphere is broken by the different continents, the bulges of South America and Africa, which look almost close enough to touch each other. Distinctive coastlines like the Iberian Peninsula or the pointed thrust of the state of Florida still stand out. And yet, as solid as the Earth appears, there is a fragility about it amid the immense darkness of outer space.

Neil can see whole weather systems moving across the planet.

"Houston," says Neil, "we're just looking at you out our window here. Looks like there's a circulation of cloud that's just moved east of Houston over the Gulf and Florida area. Did that have any rain in it this morning?"

"Roger," says Bruce. "Our report from outside says that it's raining out here, and it looks like you've got a pretty good eye for the weather there!"

A couple of hours later, there is time for broadcasting a live TV transmission. The picture is grainy and the sound is fuzzy, but the millions of people watching on Earth are amazed that the transmission can take place at all.

The first image to appear is a fuzzy one of Earth.

"You're seeing Earth," says Neil, "as we see it, out our left-hand window, just a little more than a half Earth. We're looking at the eastern Pacific Ocean, and the north half of the top half of the screen, we can see North America, Alaska, United States, Canada, Mexico, and Central America." He describes the blue cast of the oceans and the greens of the northwestern United States and

VIEWERS ON EARTH SEE A FLICKERING IMAGE OF THEIR HOME PLANET

Canada. He explains that the colors he sees are somewhat muted compared to earlier in the journey because they are now so much farther away.

When the geography lesson ends, Mike is ready to jump in. "Okay, world, hold onto your hat," he says, playfully. "I'm going to turn you upside down." And then he turns the handheld camera over to do just that.

Buzz follows with some zero-G pushups and Neil stands on his head, which is something of an achievement given the limited space available. After 35 minutes, Neil brings the show to an end. "As we pan back out to the distance at which we see the Earth," he says, "it's Apollo 11 signing off."

The last thing the viewers on Earth see is the flickering image of their home planet filling its modest spot in the Solar System.

The TV show is well received, but not all the news from home is light-hearted. NASA has learned that Apollo 11 isn't the only vehicle from Earth now heading to the Moon. Surprisingly, the Soviet Union also has a new spacecraft heading that way. There are no people on board, but this probe, Luna 15, is definitely on a mission. The question is, what kind of mission?

The Soviets aren't telling.

"There's no cause for alarm," the Soviet spokesman insists. "The orbit of probe Luna 15 does not intersect the trajectory of Apollo 11."

But that doesn't settle things, not really. No "intersection" still leaves plenty of room for mischief or worse. Is the probe designed to jam transmissions from Apollo 11? Is it meant to spy on the mission—and maybe learn some guarded secrets? Or is the probe simply meant to get to the Moon, pick up samples from the surface, and then beat the Americans home, achieving another space first?

Only time will tell.

The three astronauts say they're not concerned. (Still, they can't help but feel a little better when they later learn that Luna 15 crashes on the Moon's surface.)

ON THE THIRD DAY, THEY CLOSE IN ON THE MOON

On the third day after liftoff, they close in on the Moon itself. While much of the surface is in complete shadow, the remainder is bathed in Earthshine. This is light from the Sun that is reflecting off the Earth and illuminating the Moon, casting it in a pale blue glow. At times on their trip the Earthshine streams through the capsule windows so brightly you could read a book by it.

It's a view few other people have witnessed, the Moon this close at hand, bathed in blue light. The astronauts are highly trained and focused on the tasks they need to carry out, but sights like this remind them of the significance of their mission. If they succeed, and become the first people to set foot on another world, it will change humanity's place in the universe forever.

And the impact of their mission is underscored by the news they are now hearing from home. Bruce reads up the morning headlines. He tells the crew that they are dominating the news all over the world—even in Russia, where they are calling Neil the "Czar of the Ship." People everywhere are preparing to watch the historic event by bringing radios to work and installing TV sets in public places. Even the Pope in Rome is making special preparations—installing color TV to watch the transmission, even though Italian television is still black and white.

Now having traveled 160,000 miles from Earth, the crew won't be able to pick out Earth's land details for much longer. Soon it will be time to put the brakes on and adjust their path into the projected lunar orbit.

However, no audience back on Earth will witness this event. It will take place on the far side, or so-called dark side, of the Moon. This side is not called dark because there is less light shining on it. It is called dark simply because it remained unknown for so long, due to the fact it cannot be seen from Earth. The Moon orbits around Earth, but also rotates on its axis at the same time. By a cosmic quirk, its speed of rotation means one side always faces Earth and one side faces away.

Since the space age began, uncrewed probes have sent back pictures of the Moon's hidden face. The Soviet probe Luna 3 was the first, in 1959. It circled the Moon and took 18 images of the previously hidden landscape, revealing it for the first time. More recently the crews of Apollo 8 and Apollo 10 circled the Moon and saw the dark side with their own eyes.

Flying to the far side is a little unsettling, especially for everyone back in Mission Control. When a spacecraft goes behind the Moon, all communication with it is temporarily lost because the Moon itself

"LOOK AT THAT MOON!"

blocks transmissions to and from Earth. That means Mission Control will not know what is going on until the spacecraft safely reappears.

If the engine fails, they won't know.

If one of the astronauts has a heart attack, they won't know.

If the ship blows up, they won't know.

And even if the engine burn is completely successful, they won't know that either until Apollo 11 comes back out.

"One minute to LOS."

"Mark that," says Buzz. LOS is short for Loss of Signal.

"This is Houston," says Mission Control. "All your systems are looking good going around the corner. We'll see you on the other side. Over."

After one last crackle, silence descends on the ship.

Buzz looks at the surface in awe. It is pock-marked with craters and crevices, much more so than the more familiar side that faces Earth. This makes sense since meteors have been bombarding this side of the Moon without anything getting in their way since the Moon's creation over 4 billion years ago.

"What a spectacular view!" says Neil.

"God," says Mike, "look at that Moon!"

They see vast plains, all that is left of ancient volcanic eruptions. Channels streak the surface, the remains of later lava flows.

"Fantastic," says Neil. "Look back there behind us, sure looks like a gigantic crater; look at the mountains going around it. My gosh, they're monsters!"

"Yes," says Mike, "there's a moose down here you just wouldn't believe. There's the biggest one yet. God, it's huge! It is immense! It's so big I can't even get it in the window. You want to look at that? That's the biggest one you ever seen in your life!"

Now Mike starts the Lunar Orbit Insertion burn, which lasts about six minutes. A little later, a second burn of 17 seconds completes the change to their path, putting them in a stable orbit around the Moon.

But there is no one to share the news with. They are still on the dark side. Their family, their friends, their world, cannot be reached. Not yet.

If the astronauts feel nervous about being disconnected, they keep it to themselves. Then the radio crackles.

"Apollo 11, Apollo 11, this is Houston. Do you read? Over."

"Yes, we sure do," says Buzz. "The burn was just nominal as all get-out, and everything's looking good."

CHAPTER SIX
THE LONELIEST MAN

The proposed landing site for Neil and Buzz is a spot in the Sea of Tranquility. As the astronauts are well aware, it is not a real sea. The Moon has no water for that. But it is a fairly smooth and level area, formed when lava flowed into ancient impact craters many millions of years ago. From Earth they look like dark patches so early astronomers thought they must be seas, and that's how they got their name.

The astronauts already know a lot about their landing site. Although they will be the first human visitors to the Moon's surface, earlier unmanned probes have taken thousands of pictures of the surface, and the recent Apollo 10 mission performed a fly-by to scope out the best places for a lunar landing.

According to plan, Neil and Buzz now open the hatch and pass through the tunnel connecting the Lunar Module to the CSM. Now that the two craft are about to separate, they are given call signs to make communication easier. The Lunar Module is named *Eagle* while the CSM is *Columbia*.

The hatches are closed. Only Neil and Buzz will be going down to the surface. Mike's job is to stay behind in *Columbia*, in orbit around the Moon, ready for their return. He hits the switch that releases *Eagle* from *Columbia*. However, there is a slight difference in air pressure inside the two vehicles. When the connection is severed, this difference gives *Eagle* just a little more of a push than expected.

"I think you've got a fine-looking flying machine there, *Eagle*, despite the fact you're upside down," radios Mike.

"Somebody's upside down!" jokes Neil.

"You guys take care."

"See you later," says Neil, as though he and Buzz were doing nothing more than going out to play a round of golf.

Neil uses *Eagle*'s thrusters to move his craft safely away. He must fly *Eagle* into a lower orbit, just 9 miles above the lunar surface, then wait for Houston's signal that it is time to start their final descent.

However when the moment comes, Neil and Buzz are having communication difficulties. They cannot hear Houston giving them the go-ahead for descending to the lunar surface.

"*Eagle*, Houston," radios CAPCOM Charlie Duke. "If you read, you're good for powered descent. Over."

But the only reply is static.

So Mike, whose radio link is working fine, relays the message. "*Eagle*, this is *Columbia*. They just gave you a go for powered descent."

About 30 seconds later, Buzz finishes readjusting the radio antennae. Now, *Eagle* can communicate again with Houston.

"Keep talking to me, guys," radios Mike, a little nervously.

But that really isn't possible because in a few minutes *Columbia*'s orbit takes Mike around the curve of the Moon and back onto the dark side. For the next 48 minutes, he will be truly alone—completely

IT IS LIKE BEING ALONE IN A PITCH-BLACK OCEAN

cut off from every other living person and hundreds of thousands of miles from home.

It should be a lonely place to be, but Mike feels strangely peaceful. He's part of a team, and he knows his role is just as important as that of his crewmates. He has to stay on the alert. He doesn't know what problems Neil and Buzz may soon be facing. If they try to land and find the surface too dangerous, they may instantly blast off again. Or they may be fine for a few minutes but then see the need to quickly depart. If either of these things happen, *Eagle* will be able to catch up with *Columbia* for docking. But if *Eagle* stays down any longer than that, they will have to coordinate a more complicated docking procedure when Mike comes back around from the dark side.

Through his window he can see only stars. Where the Moon should be is just darkness—a big empty space. He thinks it is like being totally alone in the middle of a pitch-black ocean.

On his own in the inky blackness, he feels a heightened sense of awareness. As he emerges from the far side, he sees the Earth, tiny and fragile, suspended in the velvety darkness. "That shiny blue world", he thinks, "I could blot it out with my thumb."

He is eager to follow *Eagle*'s progress as it approaches the surface. Every time *Columbia*'s orbit takes Mike over where he believes they have landed, he looks for a visual sign of *Eagle*. Mike would like this reassurance because, although he has plenty to do to keep *Columbia* running smoothly, he also has a lot of time to think.

Maybe more than he would like.

For months now, Mike has been haunted by a secret fear. It's kind of a bad dream. He imagines himself in lunar orbit, waiting for news from Neil and Buzz down on the surface.

And then at last he gets the news. Bad news.

Neil and Buzz are in trouble.

The problem may be any number of things—a broken gyro, a glitchy computer, even a pilot's error. But whatever has happened, Neil and Buzz are stranded on the surface.

Now what?

Columbia has no landing gear. That means Mike has no way to land on the lunar surface. It's not a question of risking a landing. It wouldn't make a difference how much he wanted to do a rescue. It's not possible. If Neil and Buzz are unable to help themselves get off the Moon, for any reason, Mike will have no choice.

He will return to Earth alone.

And that's the nightmare.

No matter how innocent he is, and how tightly his hands are tied, Mike will be a marked man. If things go wrong for Neil and Buzz, he will spend the rest of his life feeling responsible for their deaths.

CHAPTER SEVEN
NOW OR NEVER

Neil and Buzz are not the first astronauts to fly a Lunar Module. Rusty Schweickart and James McDivitt of Apollo 9 first tested the capabilities of the Lunar Module in a low Earth orbit four months before. Then, in May, Apollo 10's Thomas Stafford and Gene Cernan had gone close to the Moon itself—piloting the Lunar Module down to about 9 miles from the surface. Now it is Neil and Buzz's time to make history. They will be the first to fly their fragile craft to the Moon's surface.

Eagle is a marvel of modern technology, but it is not about to win any beauty contests. To save weight, there is no wall paneling, so all of the wiring and plumbing are completely exposed. Buzz thinks *Eagle* has all the charm of the inside of a diesel locomotive. But at least a locomotive is tough. As near as Buzz can tell, he could jam a screwdriver through the thin cabin walls.

Neil and Buzz are both standing up inside *Eagle* because there isn't enough room for seats. Now at an altitude of 50,000 feet, they are on their way down in a vehicle that has never been tested for landing in the weak lunar gravity. It works just fine on Earth, but who knows how it will handle under such different conditions?

Whatever comes up, though, everyone in Houston is there to help. Flight Director Gene Kranz, who is currently in charge at Mission Control, makes this very clear. "From now on," he says, "no one person will enter or leave this room until we have either landed, we have crashed, or we have aborted." And just in case anyone

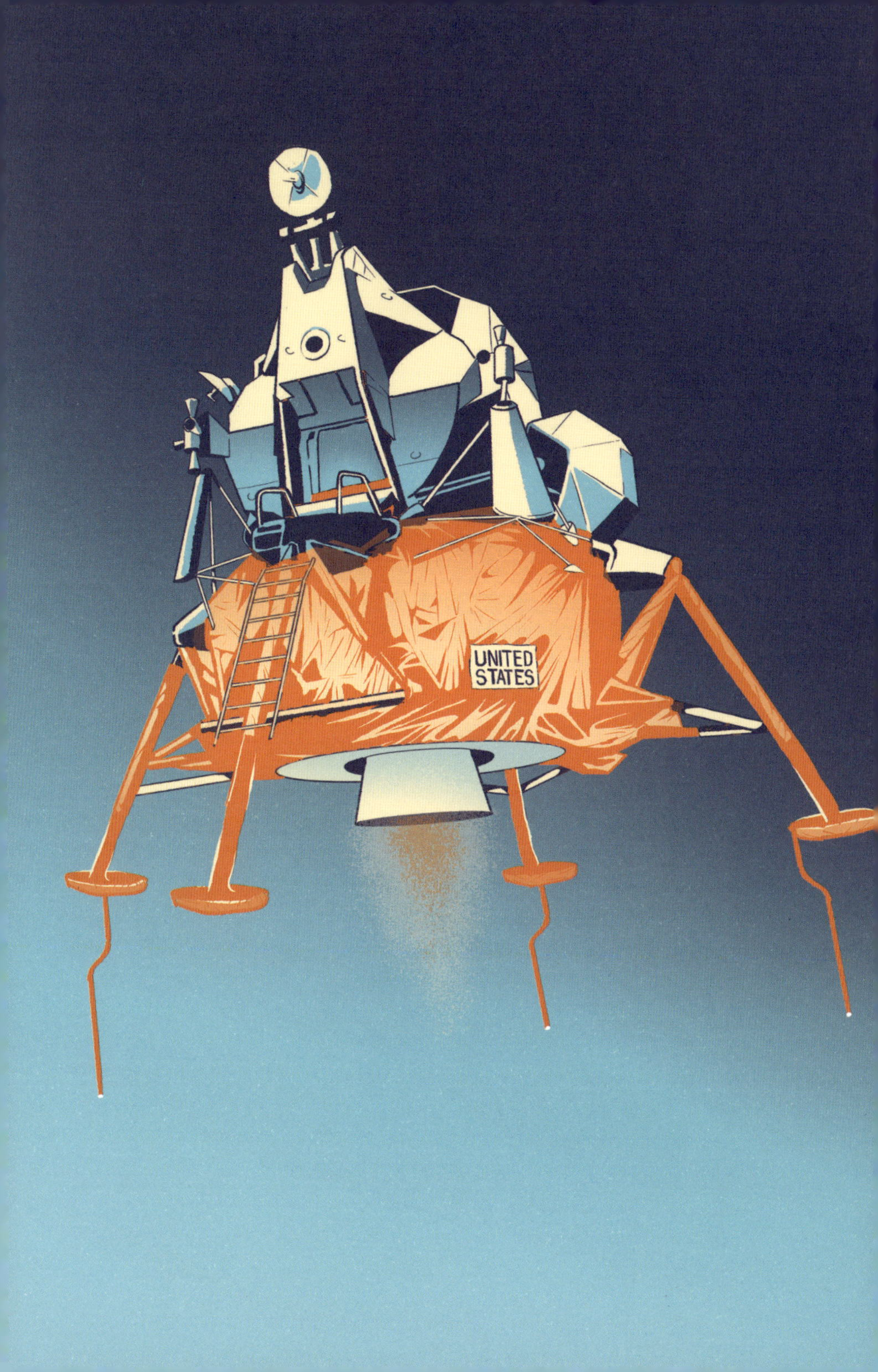
UNITED
STATES

wonders if he is really serious about this, he orders the doors leading outside to be locked.

Inside *Eagle*, Mike's voice crackles over the radio. "*Eagle*, this is *Columbia*. They just gave you a go for powered descent."

Neil pushes the PROCEED button on the guidance computer.

"Ignition," he says calmly.

ONLY THREE OUTCOMES NOW LIE AHEAD: TO ABORT, TO CRASH, OR TO MAKE A SAFE LANDING

Now *Eagle* descends from its 50,000-foot height toward the Moon, not too fast or too slow, but with careful intent. *Eagle* carries just enough fuel for one attempt. So, only three possible outcomes now lie ahead: to abort, to crash, or to make a safe landing.

Neil is getting his first view of the landing approach, passing over Taruntius crater. The pictures and maps brought back by Apollos 8 and 10 had shown what it would look like, and it does look like those images. But seeing it with his own eyes is something different—like the difference between being at a football game and watching one on TV.

However, as Neil continues scanning the lunar surface, he begins to frown. Something is wrong. The landmarks he memorized from all the long hours in the simulator are the right ones. But they are not appearing at the right time. He is recognizing landmarks about two seconds ahead of when he should be seeing them. Two seconds may not matter in many situations, but it does here. At the speed they are traveling, those seconds mean they will be miles off course when they attempt a landing.

He doesn't know it until later, but the reason they are ahead is the tiny extra push *Eagle* got when decoupling from *Columbia*. Their increased speed has put them ahead of schedule. Meanwhile, the descent engine, which Neil is not controlling, is throttling down as programmed, unaware that *Eagle* is out of sync with the programming. Overshooting the landing site is enough to deal with, but there's more.

Suddenly, a frozen display on the computer reads "1202."

"Program alarm," says Neil. For the first time in the mission he sounds worried.

Buzz nods.

It's an error code, they understand that. What they don't understand is what the error code is for. Everything on board *Eagle* seems fine.

Suddenly, *Eagle*'s master alarm sounds off.

Back on Earth, the same alarms are heard.

"*Beeep … Beeep … Beeep …*"

Neil remains calm. He's trained for this. But calm is not the same as unconcerned.

"Give us a reading on the 1202 program alarm," he asks Houston.

Hundreds of people in Mission Control stand ready to answer any questions he has. But in this case, nobody has a good explanation. They think the computer may be overloaded. If that's true, it will need a reboot to start over. But if a reboot is needed, the mission guidelines are very clear about what comes next.

Abort.

The mission must be aborted during a reboot because the computer won't be available to help navigate the landing.

And yet … the computer appears to be working fine—even if the alarm says it's not. So, unless the situation changes again, the experts in Houston decide *Eagle* should keep going. It's a risk, of course, but it still seems like the best option.

Buzz monitors the control panels as the lander begins its descent. His job is to give Neil regular read-outs of their altitude and speed—all his attention is focused on the console in front of him. Neil's eyes are fixed ahead, scanning the alien gray landscape below.

Just 10 minutes to go.

HE IS RECOGNIZING LANDMARKS ABOUT TWO SECONDS AHEAD OF WHEN HE SHOULD BE SEEING THEM …

The radio crackles with static as the signal between Mission Control and *Eagle* drops in and out. "You are go," says Mission Control. "Go to continue powered descent!"

Lower and lower *Eagle* descends. The astronauts are close now, so near they can see the ship's shadow on the surface below.

But wait! At that moment, Neil frowns again. The auto-targeting is taking them right into a football-field-sized crater, strewn with big

boulders and rocks. Landing there will be a disaster, for sure. The flimsy *Eagle* isn't built to survive a rough landing. It will smash on the rocks.

Neil's eyes flick down to the fuel gauge. Its red light is blinking. They are nearly out of fuel. For the first time in the whole mission, Neil's heart begins to race.

He takes a deep breath, then grips the controls even more firmly. He knows what he must do. There's no time to check with Houston.

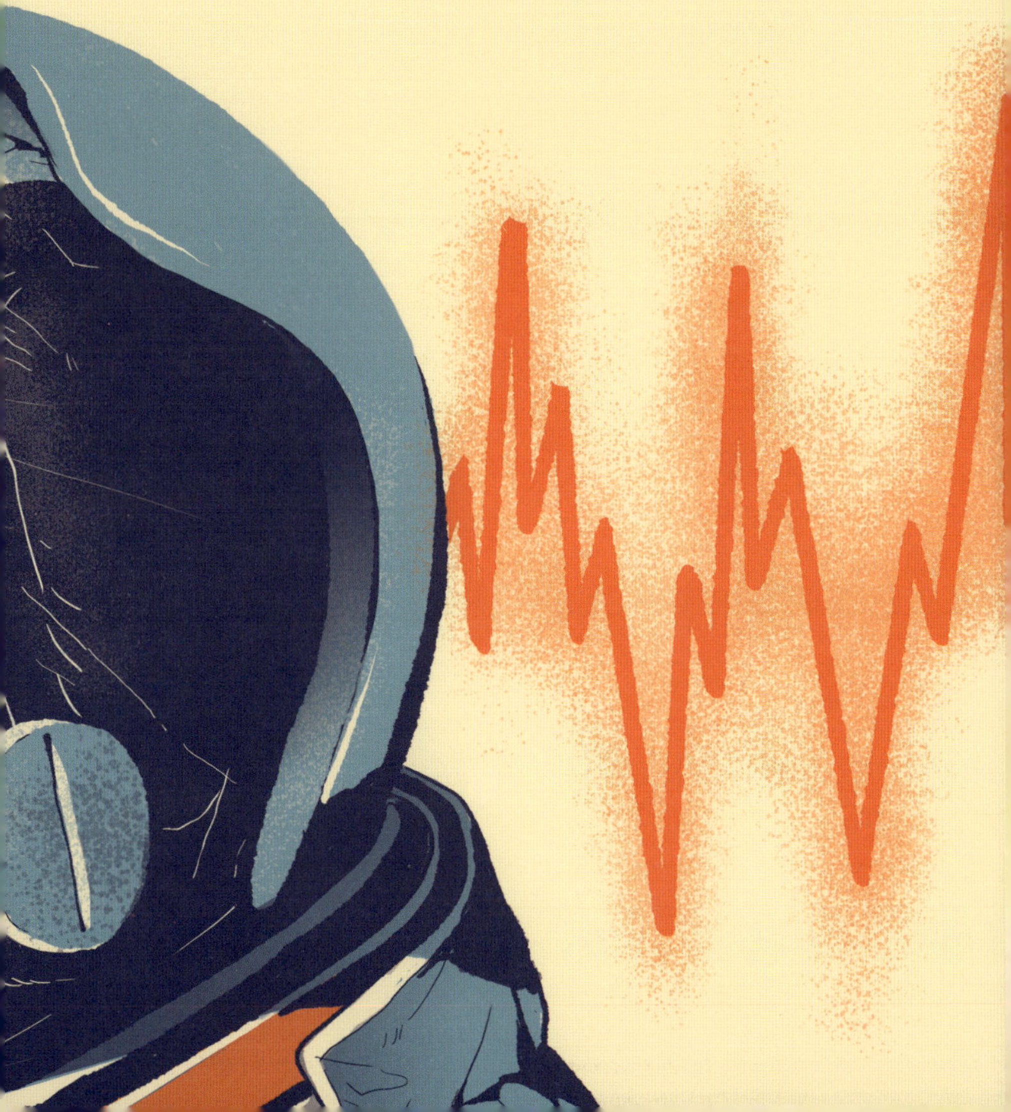

No time for second-guessing. Neil must override the computer and land *Eagle* himself. He takes a deep breath and grips the controls.

He is already thinking ahead ... When the fuel gauge indicates five percent remaining, that means he will have 90 seconds of flying time left before dropping onto the surface or deciding to abort. How close does he have to be to the surface to drop down safely? 25 feet? Easy. 40 feet? A bit rocky, but still okay. 70 feet? Well, he and Buzz may survive the landing, but *Eagle* may be so damaged it will never fly again.

Which would leave them trapped on the Moon. Forever.

They are still 400 feet above the lunar surface. Houston stays quiet, trying to let Neil and Buzz concentrate.

"100 feet," says Buzz. "Five percent fuel remaining."

Neil frowns again. Time is running out. And the fuel gauge will soon be too low to measure how little is left.

Neil slows *Eagle* as much as he can. He has to land in a dead drop. Any forward momentum, and its delicate legs will snap like twigs.

"Okay," says Buzz. "75 feet. And it's looking good."

But they are still moving forward at a speed of 20 feet per second.

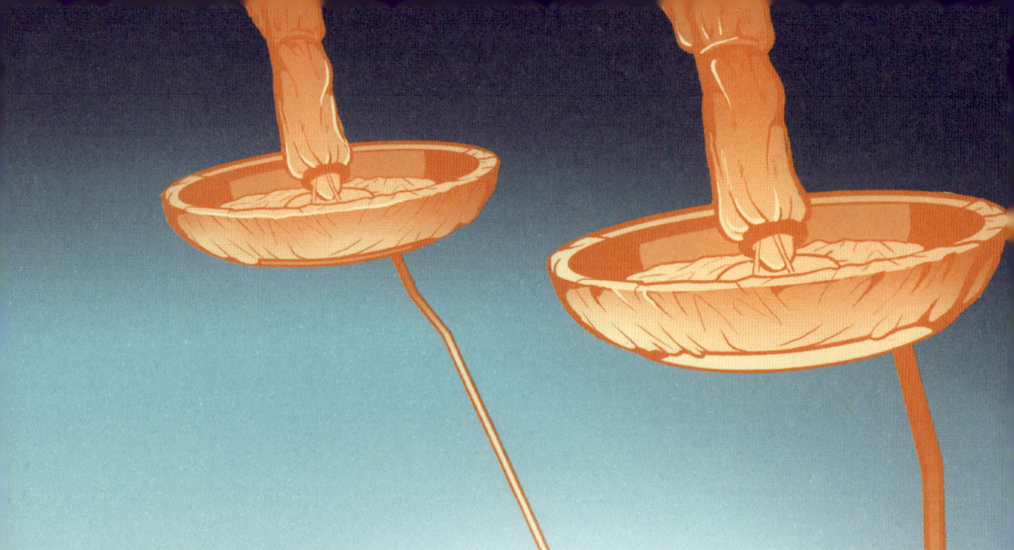

"30 feet," says Buzz.

Finally, Neil finds his landing spot. Once he gets closer he can no longer see it exactly because the descent engine is kicking up too much dust. But he's confident it's there.

A few seconds later, first contact is made.

There are landing probes 5 feet long connected to *Eagle*'s footpads. When they make contact with the surface a light comes on inside the capsule.

"Contact light," says Buzz, when he sees the light illuminate.

Then the landing gear touches down a moment later and *Eagle*, like a stately bird, settles gently onto the Moon.

"Okay," says Buzz. "Engine Stop."

They are miles from the originally predicted touchdown. But neither Neil nor Buzz are worrying about getting style points for their efforts.

They are down and they are intact. "Houston," says Neil, "Tranquility Base here. The *Eagle* has landed."

"TRANQUILITY BASE HERE.
THE EAGLE HAS LANDED."

CHAPTER EIGHT
FIRST STEPS

The applause at Mission Control is pretty loud even if it doesn't quite reach up to the Moon itself.

"Tranquility," says CAPCOM Charlie Duke from Houston. "Be advised there're lots of smiling faces in this room and all over the world. Over."

"Well," says Neil, "there are two of them up here."

"That was a beautiful job, you guys," says Charlie.

"And don't forget one in the Command Module ..." says Mike from high overhead in *Columbia*. "It sure sounded great from up here. You guys did a fantastic job."

"Thank you," says Neil. "Just keep that orbiting base ready for us up there now."

"Will do," says Mike.

As Neil and Buzz look out the window, they face a grayish-white level plain, pock-marked with craters. The craters range in size from 1 to 2 feet wide all the way up to 50 feet. Their edges look sharp and forbidding. There is nothing welcoming about them.

There's an eerie feeling to the scene, without a breath of wind or hint of color to soften the ominous impression. It's a landscape millions of years in the making, where no human being has ever ventured before.

Neil can also see the Earth above the horizon, and it looks big, bright, and beautiful. The contrast with the dry, lifeless Moon is certainly striking.

With the drama of the landing behind them, thoughts immediately turn to more practical matters. Such as figuring out exactly where they are. Luckily, although they didn't land at their intended site, they are hardly lost. And they have the team in Houston to help confirm their location. It turns out that they are about 4 miles west of where they planned to be, but still well within the Sea of Tranquility.

The flight plan now calls for the astronauts to take a four-hour rest break. Forget about that. Both Neil and Buzz are too excited to wait, although they do manage to have a bite to eat.

The lunar extravehicular activity (EVA) is the focal point of the whole mission. The astronauts will step out of the Lunar Module and finally set foot on the Moon's surface. They won't spend long outside the spacecraft—a few hours at most—but they have a lengthy task-list to accomplish. They will take samples of Moon rock and deploy three science experiments: one to study the solar wind, one to measure moonquakes, and one intended to calculate the exact distance between the Moon and the Earth.

But getting ready for the big moment means more than just throwing on a jacket and tying their shoes. The Moon is a place of environmental extremes—very hot during the day and very cold at night. And there's no atmosphere on the Moon, since the gravity is too weak to hold a blanket of gases in place. This means there's no air to breathe, and no air pressure—only the vacuum of space.

To survive in this deadly lunar environment then, the astronauts have to put on EVA suits and life-support packs. The Portable Life Support System is the latest marvel in NASA's inventory. It was first used by Rusty Schweickart during his spacewalk on Apollo 9's mission four months earlier. Each pack can support a human being for hours, providing air and water and a comfortable operating temperature.

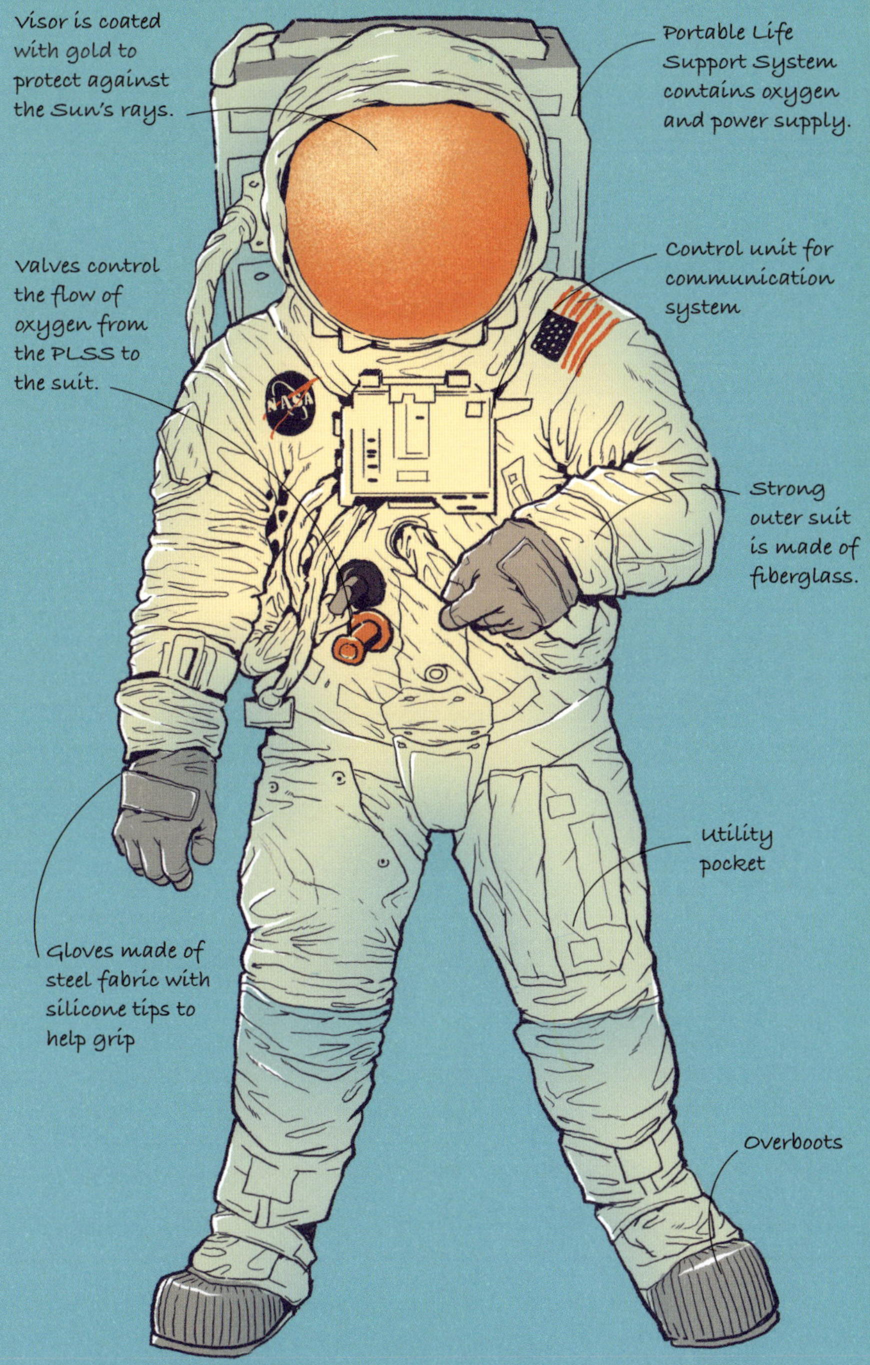
Visor is coated with gold to protect against the Sun's rays.
Portable Life Support System contains oxygen and power supply.
Control unit for communication system
Valves control the flow of oxygen from the PLSS to the suit.
NASA
Strong outer suit is made of fiberglass.
Utility pocket
Gloves made of steel fabric with silicone tips to help grip
Overboots

This is pretty amazing since just inches away, outside their suits, the temperature is either 260°F in the sunlight or about -40°F in the shade. The suit is pressurized, which means it is inflated with oxygen to mimic the air pressure that exists on Earth. Without this pressure, the astronauts' body fluids would boil in the vacuum of space.

Unfortunately, none of that technology is helpful in actually putting the suit on. And both astronauts have to be wearing their suits before they can depressurize *Eagle*'s cabin and go outside. Until now the spacecraft has been filled with oxygen, so that the astronauts can breathe and to provide the air pressure their bodies are used to. This gas must be vented slowly before opening the cabin door. Depressurizing rapidly by simply opening the door would cause a catastrophic explosion.

HE BEGINS MAKING HIS WAY DOWN THE LADDER

There are shoulder harnesses to adjust and waist harnesses to clip. Once the helmet and gloves are put on, the pack's oxygen, water, and umbilical hoses need to be connected. There is so little space inside *Eagle* that Neil and Buzz take turns getting dressed.

But finally, everything that must be done has been done. The moment has come.

As Mission Commander, Neil has the honor of leaving *Eagle* first. He could be nervous about somehow tearing his suit or having his oxygen flow blocked or a hundred other dangers, but none of these things are foremost in his mind at the moment. What he has come to realize is that the first words he will speak on the Moon are a cause of great national and international interest.

The bulky suit makes it hard to exit the craft gracefully. Neil manages to back out on all fours, getting advice from Buzz along the way.

"All right," says Buzz. "Move ... to your ... roll to the left. Okay. Now you're clear ... Put your left foot to the right a little bit. Okay. That's good. Roll left. Good."

And then he begins making his way down the ladder. On his way down, he pulls a handle to open a compartment tucked behind the ladder, revealing

a TV camera. In grainy black-and-white images, his next movements will be broadcast to 600 million people back on Earth.

And so, at 10:56 pm EDT on July 20, 1969, Neil drops down onto the lunar surface.

"THAT'S ONE SMALL STEP FOR MAN, ONE GIANT LEAP FOR MANKIND"

"That's one small step for man," Neil radios back to Houston. "One giant leap for mankind."

The surface is made of rock, strewn with fragments of different sizes, and coated with dust. It looks like a very fine powder, made of tiny grains. It sticks to Neil's boots, smudging like charcoal. For centuries, people joked that the Moon was made of cheese. No one ever really believed this but on the other hand no one knows what it really is made from, either. The precious samples from Apollo 11 will let scientists study Moon rock for the first time, and begin to unlock the secrets of how the Moon formed in the first place.

Houston reminds Neil to collect a sample from the surface as soon as possible in case an emergency develops, and they have to leave in a hurry. He scoops a bagful of rocks and dust, and stashes it in a pocket on the leg of his suit.

A few minutes later, Buzz joins him on the surface.

"Beautiful view!" he says.

Neil agrees. "Isn't that something? Magnificent sight out here."

"Magnificent desolation," Buzz replies.

It's daytime on the Moon and the Sun is shining, but the sky is totally black, because there is no atmosphere to scatter the light. The gray surface seems dazzling and the shadows are pin-sharp. But the astronauts can't take too much time to admire the view because their time on the Moon is short and scheduled.

The pressure suits are cumbersome, making moving around slightly challenging. No one had known what to expect from the Moon's low gravity—about one-sixth of the gravity on Earth. But they find it quite easy to get used to. Buzz thinks it's a little like being on a trampoline. He experiments with different ways of moving around: a bouncing walk from one leg to the other, then small, kangaroo-like hops.

Next, Buzz sets up an experiment called the Solar Wind Collector. It uses a sheet of aluminum foil supported by a frame to gather

particles streaming off the Sun. This will let scientists study what this solar wind is made from for the first time. The Moon is the perfect place for this experiment, since it has no atmosphere and no magnetic field to deflect the particles.

After that, they plant an American flag in the dirt. With no air on the Moon to make the flag flutter, the flag is mounted on a crossbar to keep it open.

Soon, they take a break to receive a call from Richard Nixon, the President of the United States.

"THIS HAS TO BE THE MOST HISTORIC PHONE CALL EVER MADE"

"Hello, Neil and Buzz," he says. "I'm talking to you from the Oval Room in the White House, and this certainly has to be the most historic phone call ever made. I just can't tell you how proud we all are." The president says their mission on Tranquility Base should be an inspiration to people on Earth to work toward peace and tranquility at home.

"Thank you, Mr. President," says Neil. "It's a great honor and privilege for us to be here."

The longest-distance telephone call in history is broadcast live on television and seen by people all over the world. Once the call ends, the astronauts get back to their mission. As Neil roams around, he makes sure he collects a wide variety of rock samples from the surface.

Buzz adds to their collection by taking some core samples from beneath the surface. He does this by pounding a hollow tube down into the surface and then pulling it out. Unfortunately, driving the tube with the necessary force isn't easy, even when starting with the geology hammer above his head.

Still, whatever they do, they don't go very far doing it. Both Neil and Buzz always stay within about 300 feet, the length of a football field, of *Eagle*.

Eventually, after activating all the equipment they brought to the surface it is time to leave. Buzz reenters *Eagle* after spending exactly 93 minutes outside it. Neil then passes along all of the things they have collected to be stowed away. Once this is done, he maneuvers back inside, again with Buzz's help.

"Just keep your head down close. Now start arching your back. That's good. Plenty of room. Okay now, all right, arch your back a little … Roll right just a little bit. Head down."

"Thank you," says Neil. "Am I bumping now?"

"No, you're clear," says Buzz.

"Okay," says Neil.

"Turn right," says Buzz. "That's right … Okay. Now move your foot, and I'll get the hatch."

Finally, a little more than two and a half hours after it starts, the EVA is over. The hatch is closed and locked.

As *Eagle* repressurizes, both astronauts laugh. They had been told that there was a chance that the lunar dust on their suits might catch fire when exposed to oxygen inside the Lunar Module. When they remove the EVA suits, they find the dust smears easily over everything it touches and has a distinctive smell that reminds them of burnt gunpowder or charcoal.

For their final meal on the Moon, Neil and Buzz enjoy beef stew, bacon cubes, peaches, and date fruitcake. Then it's time to take out the trash. They put their helmets and gloves back on and connect themselves to *Eagle*'s support system before throwing out to the surface anything they no longer need—even their expensive backpacks and cameras. Any extra weight may become an issue for returning to space, so if they no longer need it—simple or complicated, expensive or cheap—it is left behind.

Eight hours later, after 21 hours and 36 minutes on the Moon, and a cramped night of little sleep, they are ready to go. Checklists complete, they strap themselves in for the big moment.

"You're cleared for takeoff," says Houston.

Buzz nods. "Number one on the runway," he says.

His countdown is no match for the dramatic one they heard a few days earlier when they left Earth, but it is just as important.

AS EAGLE RISES, SPARKS FLY

"Nine, eight, seven, six, five, abort stage, engine arm, ascent, proceed."

Neil keys the computer, directing the little explosives beneath them to open the helium tanks, sending the compressed gas into the ascent engine. The connecting harness between the ascent engine and the descent engine is severed.

As *Eagle* rises, leaving its landing gear behind, sparks fly and dust from the lunar surface is kicked up. On the front of the landing gear, just behind the ladder, is a small plaque. Underneath the two hemispheres of Earth its inscription reads:

Here men from the planet Earth first set foot upon the Moon,
July 1969 A.D. We came in peace for all mankind.

CHAPTER NINE
HOMEWARD BOUND

Nobody, not even Neil or Buzz, is more delighted than Mike that the *Eagle* has made it off the lunar surface.

He has completed 11 lunar orbits during the roughly 21 hours his crewmates have spent on the Moon. And he is not done yet because more orbits will pass before *Eagle* and *Columbia* can be reunited.

Of course, Neil and Buzz are also still holding their breaths at least a little. As *Eagle* climbs through the lunar sky, it wobbles slightly because the fuel tanks are mounted on each side, and as they empty, *Eagle*'s balance is off for a short time. The ascent engine must burn for a little over seven minutes to provide the necessary altitude and speed to reach orbit. If they don't get this right, the mission may be doomed even now.

Once *Eagle* reaches a lunar orbit, that's a big step forward. But another task awaits. *Eagle* must now chase down *Columbia* in order to dock with it again. To do that, its radar communicates with a transponder on *Columbia*. Over the next 3 hours and 40 minutes, *Eagle*'s thrusters burn several times to bring the two spacecraft closer together.

A final burn aligns the two craft on a single course. As *Columbia*'s pilot, it's now Mike's turn to take over.

"I see you don't have any landing gear," he radios to Neil and Buzz.

Neil answers in the same spirit. "It's good you're not confused on which end to dock with," he says back.

Clearly, they are both very happy to be almost together again.

Mike nods and begins to guide them closer. "That's the way, keep going … go a little bit more … go ahead, go ahead … Okay, stop. Okay, I have it now."

Columbia and *Eagle* now touch. Two capture latches are activated, and Mike flips a switch that fires a small blast, pulling the two spacecraft together.

But what happens next is a surprise—and not a pleasant one. Mike is expecting a sleepy *Eagle*, one that he can easily corral into place. Instead, he gets a wild bird trying to break free. The two ships are not quite aligned right, and *Eagle* is trying to retract itself from *Columbia* to start the link again.

Mike works harder, wrestling with his controller. This is no nightmare, he tells himself, just a bump in the road.

Finally, he steers the two craft back together.

Then the docking is sealed.

Four hours after leaving the Moon, Neil and Buzz hear the reassuring sound of the latches clanging shut above their heads.

Mike leaves his couch and drifts forward to open the hatch. As he does so, Neil and Buzz are waiting for him. Mike grabs Buzz's hand in a firm grasp of welcome, and Buzz's smile gives away everything he's thinking. Then Neil accepts a similar greeting. They made it! Whatever happens next, the crew is back together again.

Now Buzz and Neil pass up all their precious lunar rock samples and photographic film through the hatch. Soon they will leave *Eagle* for the last time. However, Neil and Buzz take a moment to tidy up a little. It's a sentimental gesture because they both know *Eagle* will never be used again. Still, they want to show some respect for the tremendous job the craft has done. There were many opportunities for *Eagle* to let them down, but it came through with flying colors.

THE HATCH IS OPEN … THE CREW IS BACK TOGETHER AGAIN

Finally reentering *Columbia,* they close the hatch for the last time. Without further ceremony, they jettison *Eagle* into space.

"There she goes," says Mike.

By their reckoning, *Eagle* will continue to orbit until one day crashing onto the Moon's surface.

"Houston, this is *Columbia,*" says Mike. "Reading you loud and clear. We're all three back inside. The hatch is installed. We're running a pressure check—leak check. Everything's going well."

"Roger, *Columbia*," says Duke. "We copy. You guys are speedy." There are still more preparations to make before heading for home. So, it is several hours later that Mission Control gives *Columbia* the go-ahead for the trans-Earth injection (TEI). The engine will burn for two and a half minutes, increasing their velocity enough to escape lunar orbit—and send them home.

They take some farewell photographs of the Moon before receiving their next command from Houston. "This is the original CAPCOM," says Director of Flight Crew Operations Deke Slayton from Houston. "Congratulations on an outstanding job. You guys have really put on a great show up there. I think it's about time you powered down and got a little rest, however. You've had a mighty long day here. Hope you're all going to get a good sleep on the way back."

When they wake 10 hours later they have almost reached the point, 38,800 miles from the Moon, where the Moon's gravitational pull gives way to the much stronger gravitational pull from Earth—even though they are still 174,00 miles from home.

A few hours later they make a midcourse correction using *Columbia*'s thrusters. This maneuver slightly changes their flight trajectory to improve their entry path into Earth's atmosphere. It is vitally important that their trajectory be spot-on. Anything less and the spacecraft may bounce off the atmosphere, but enter too steeply and the crippling forces could tear their ship apart.

With time to spare till the splashdown the next day, the astronauts prepare for their final TV transmission to Earth. Millions of people across dozens of countries watch as they go live that night at 7:04 pm Eastern time.

"Good evening," says Neil. "This is the commander of Apollo 11. One hundred years ago, Jules Verne wrote a book about a voyage to the Moon. His spaceship, *Columbia*, took off from Florida and landed in the Pacific Ocean after completing a trip to the Moon. It seems appropriate to us to share with you some of the reflections of the crew on the modern-day *Columbia* as it completes its rendezvous with the planet Earth and the same Pacific Ocean tomorrow."

"This trip may have looked to you simple or easy," says Mike. "I'd like to assure you that has not been the case." He describes all the many pieces of machinery and equipment they have relied on during their voyage, and how they've always had total faith that they would work how they should. He pays tribute to all the people on the ground who contributed to the mission. "This operation is somewhat like the periscope of a submarine. All you see is the three of us, but beneath the surface are thousands and thousands of others, and to all those, I would like to say, thank you very much."

"This has been far more than three men on a voyage to the Moon," says Buzz. "More than the efforts of a government and industry team; more even than the efforts of one nation. We feel that this stands as a symbol of the insatiable curiosity of all mankind to explore the unknown."

The full transmission lasts 18 minutes and Neil has the honor of finishing it up. "We would like to give a special thanks to all of those Americans who built the spacecraft; who did the construction, design, the tests; put their hearts and all their abilities into those crafts. To those people tonight, we give a special thank you, and to all the other people that are listening and watching tonight, God bless you. Good night from Apollo 11."

CHAPTER TEN
SPLASHDOWN!

Neil, Buzz, and Mike all know that safely returning to Earth from space is not easy. It has been done a number of times, but almost all of the descents have started from Earth orbit. Only two, Apollo 8 and 10, have come from a greater distance—in both cases, the Moon. Returning from the Moon makes a big difference in speed. Measurements and timing have to be even more precise for everything to go well.

Meeting the atmosphere at 24,000 miles per hour is a tricky business. The entry angle has to be exactly right, or the ship will burn up. With that hurdle cleared, another thing that has to go right is the weather. Often it cooperates, but there are no guarantees. And since astronauts can't change the weather, sometimes they have to work around it.

Which Apollo 11 suddenly has to do.

CAPCOM Charlie Duke gives Mike the update. "The weather is clobbering in at our targeted landing point due to scattered thunderstorms. We don't want to tangle with one of those, so we're going to move you."

These scattered thunderstorms are actually what is more ominously called a "screaming eagle thunderstorm," because its shape resembles that of an eagle in flight. The screaming part comes from what these storms can generate—strong winds, large hail, and even tornadoes.

Nobody wants to change flight trajectories at this point in a mission, but the prospect of a screaming eagle engulfing *Columbia* is much worse.

Houston has already picked a new site that is convenient for the fleet of ships headed by the USS *Hornet* which is waiting in the water.

Mike changes Apollo 11's trajectory to match the new target. He's feeling pretty relaxed because when Houston asks him to check on a procedure, he's not in a hurry.

"I'm right in the middle of my orange juice," he says. "Be with you in about 5 minutes."

Just before reentry, with his orange juice squared away, Mike prepares to turn the spacecraft to its proper orientation. But before he does that, he has to release the Service Module.

"That old Service Module has taken good care of us," says Mike.

"It sure has, hasn't it?" says Houston.

"It's been a champ," says Mike.

Neil and Buzz couldn't agree more. Whether or not the equipment works properly is of life-and-death importance to them, and the Service Module has performed magnificently.

Still, it's time for it to go, and Mike makes it happen. He sends a command to the well-named Service Module Jettison Controller. This starts a timer that will soon trigger the jets on the Service Module to move it away from *Columbia*. More blasts are fired to complete the separation. All that remains of the spacecraft now is the tiny conical Command Module.

USS HORNET IS WAITING IN THE WATER

Now Mike turns his attention back to *Columbia*, rotating the spacecraft so that the capsule's wide blunt base is pointed down. Entering the atmosphere blunt-end first creates more drag, slowing the capsule down more quickly. This side of the spacecraft has a protective heat shield made of steel. It is designed to burn away in layers to protect the rest of the craft. Soon 5,000°F of heat will be blasting the spaceship and only the heat shield can give the crew a chance of surviving it.

At 11:30 am on July 24, Apollo 11 starts to descend through the Earth's outer atmosphere. It collides with the thin air at around 400,000 feet from the surface.

As the spacecraft tears through the atmosphere at blistering speed, the air cannot move out of the way quickly enough. A cushion of air is compressed in front of the spacecraft and heats up to metal-melting temperatures. The cockpit is flooded with light, as the blazing gases are deflected by the heat shield and lick around the sides of the craft.

THE COCKPIT IS FLOODED WITH LIGHT AS BLAZING GASES ARE DEFLECTED BY THE HEAT SHIELD

That's perfectly normal, but it creates a communication blackout that lasts for almost four minutes. Can the astronauts survive this final challenge during the heat of reentry?

All everyone in Houston and around the world can do is wait. On board the USS *Hornet*, everything from radar to the naked eye scans the skies for a sign of the returning capsule.

Minutes pass. And then, finally, the capsule, dangling from its three parachutes, is spotted. The *Hornet* dispatches the rescue helicopters from its flight deck.

"Apollo 11, Apollo 11. This is *Hornet*. *Hornet*. Over."

"Hello, *Hornet*," says Neil. "This is Apollo 11 reading you loud and clear."

A short while later, the capsule hits the water hard about 940 miles southwest of Honolulu, Hawaii.

Columbia plunges under the surface and then comes up bobbing. The winds are blowing at about 20 miles per hour and the waves around the capsule are cresting at just a few feet.

All three astronauts have taken anti-motion-sickness pills just in case the seas are rougher than expected. The last thing anyone wants at this point is to throw up inside a sealed spacesuit.

And in fact, it is good to be careful. The waves have turned *Columbia* over. It is now floating upside down.

"Everyone okay inside," radios Neil. "Our checklist is complete. Awaiting swimmers."

It's true that the three astronauts are okay if not perfectly comfortable. They are hanging from the straps of their seats. However, they're still in a position to start motorized pumps that will inflate three specially designed air bags. Ten minutes later, these air-filled bags will turn the spacecraft back over.

"Tell everybody, take your sweet time," says Mike. "We're doing just fine in here."

EPILOGUE

Mike may say not to hurry, but the recovery forces are in no mood to dally. At the first sighting of the capsule's parachutes, Navy helicopters take off. They head for *Columbia* as fast as their rotors can turn.

Every minute of the recovery is broadcast around the world. The USS *Hornet* is about 13 miles away, but within minutes, a diver from the closest helicopter to leave the ship has attached a sea collar to keep *Columbia* from drifting. A few minutes after that the hatch is opened.

However, the astronauts do not step out. Instead, three specially sealed bio-suits are thrown in. It's possible that the astronauts may have brought back unwelcome visitors from the Moon, some kind of germs or parasites that can wreak havoc on Earth.

Better to be safe than sorry.

To guard against this development, the astronauts will spend the next three weeks in quarantine—first on board the *Hornet* and later in a specially designed trailer back in Texas. During this time, they will be examined and evaluated to make sure that they are free of contamination. Could the hazardous germs have already escaped into Earth's atmosphere during the few moments earlier when the hatch was open? Yes, but this was the best option available. Fortunately, it turns out that the only germs the astronauts carried back to Earth were the ones that they took with them into space.

One other task the astronauts perform is dealing with some government bureaucracy. After all, after leaving the United States, they visited foreign soil. Upon their return, customs officials drew

up paperwork—perhaps as a joke. The form states their place of departure as "Moon" and declares their cargo as "Moon rock and Moon dust samples."

The success of Apollo 11 fueled six further journeys of the Apollo program. Apollo 13 suffered an explosion during its voyage but still made it safely back to Earth. The other Apollos—12, 14, 15, 16, and 17—all successfully went to the Moon and back.

However, starting in the mid 1970s, support for the idea of landing people on the Moon sharply declined. Budget cuts prompted NASA to cancel future Apollo missions and shift its focus to developing the Space Shuttle, a reusable spacecraft that allowed for more frequent launches. In the 1990s, work began on an orbiting research base called the International Space Station, and the Shuttle was key to building it.

More recently, though, interest in the Moon has resurfaced. Part of this interest comes from new players in the quest to explore space, private companies such as SpaceX and Blue Origin. They have developed reusable rockets, new kinds of satellites, and stirred up the prospects of tourism for people who can afford the trip.

NASA has also stepped back into the picture. The Artemis program has an ambitious agenda to return to the Moon in the next few years. It will be testing cutting-edge technologies that will allow visits to other destinations such as the planet Mars.

As for Neil Armstrong, Buzz Aldrin, and Mike Collins, once they returned to Earth in *Columbia*, their time in space was done. However, they remain celebrated now and forever for their brave accomplishments over the 953,054 miles they traveled during those 8 days, 3 hours, 18 minutes, and 35 seconds in July 1969.

WHAT HAPPENED NEXT?

Neil Armstrong (1930–2012)

For a time after his return from the Moon, Neil was perhaps the most famous person on Earth. But he had no interest in being a celebrity, and after several years with a desk job at NASA, he took a job teaching engineering at the University of Cincinnati. Far removed from the spotlight, he died of complications from heart surgery in 2012.

Edwin "Buzz" Aldrin (1930–)

Buzz Aldrin had some difficult years, mentally and physically, adjusting to life following the Apollo 11 mission. But he rekindled his love for space flight, designing rockets and an innovative space station design. He is now in his mid-nineties and no doubt his grandchild enjoys knowing that Buzz Lightyear, the character in the Toy Story movies, is named for him.

Michael Collins (1930–2021)

Michael Collins left NASA about six months after his historic flight and later became the director of the National Air and Space Museum in Washington, D.C. In 1980, he began a new phase of his career as an aerospace consultant. Collins also wrote several books based on his experiences as an astronaut. He died after battling cancer in 2021.

About the author

Stephen Krensky has published over 200 books for children, including biographies of Leonardo da Vinci and Benjamin Franklin, historical books on Pearl Harbor and the 1849 California gold rush, as well as scientific books on magnetism and the weather. He remembers watching the Apollo 11 moon landing on television as it happened and how amazing that moment was at the time.

About the illustrator

Dr. Greta Samuel is an award-winning illustrator and comic artist. She graduated from the Academy of Fine Arts in Warsaw and holds a PhD from the Polish-Japanese Academy, specializing in drawing, visual storytelling, and contemporary illustration techniques.

About the consultant

Dr. David Whitehouse has a doctorate in astrophysics from Jodrell Bank Radio Observatory. He started his career as an astronomer and went on to become the BBC's science correspondent. He is now an author and expert on space exploration. Asteroid 4036 Whitehouse is named after him.

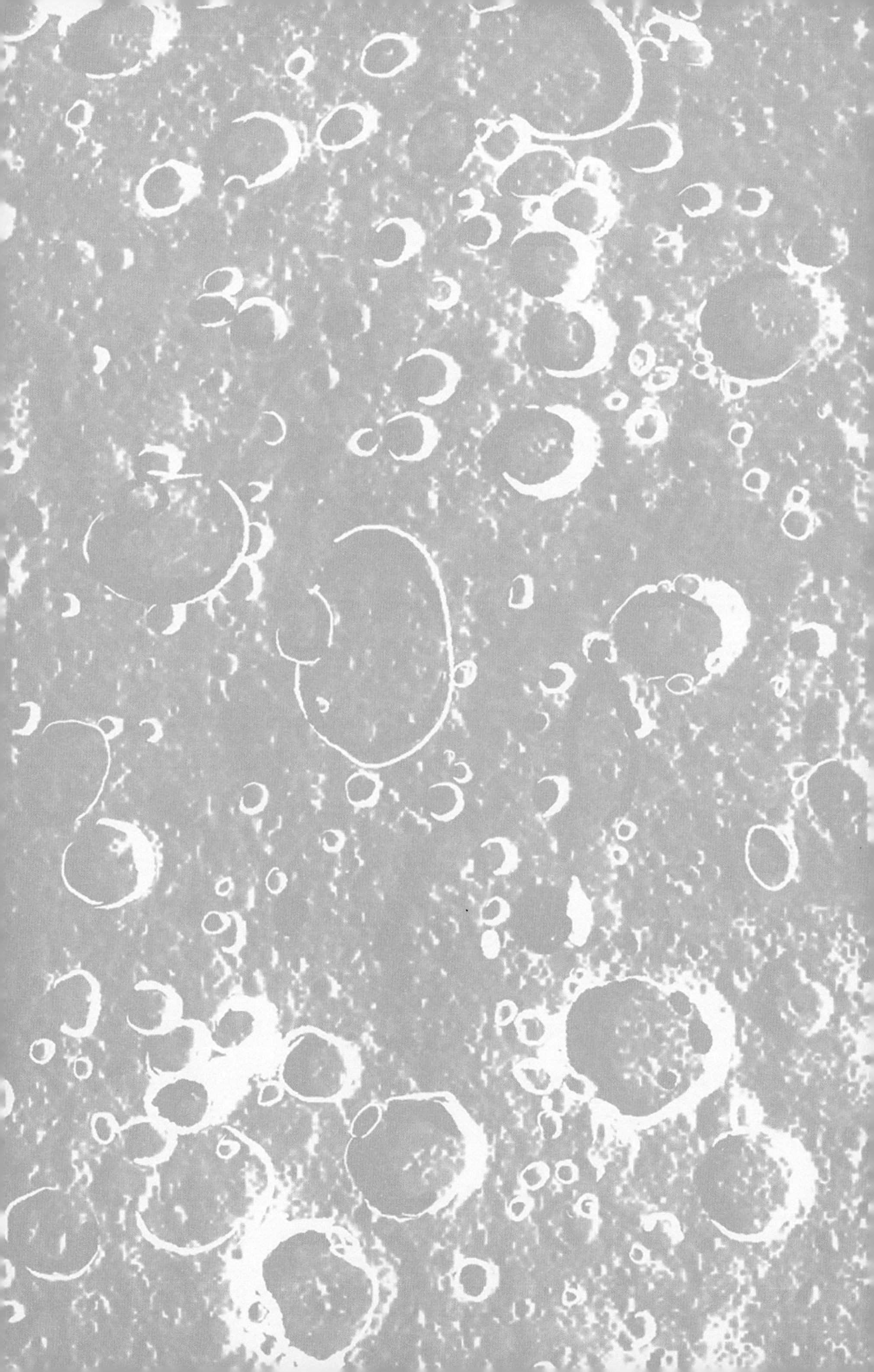

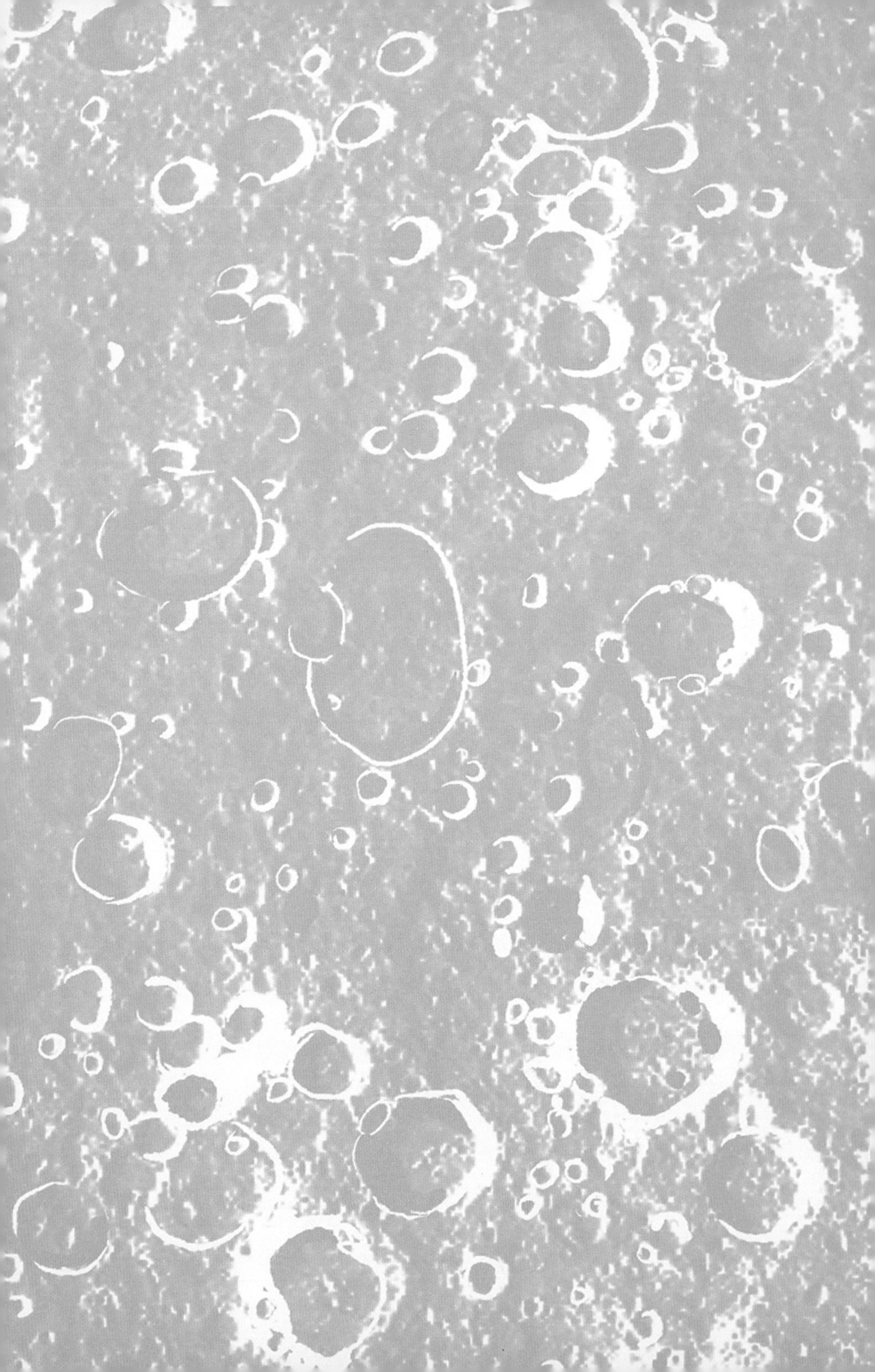